A Partnership in Literacy

A Partnership in Literacy

Teacher Education in an Urban School

Camille A. Allen
Salve Regina University

HEINEMANN
Portsmouth, NH

Heinemann
A division of Reed Elsevier Inc.
361 Hanover Street
Portsmouth, NH 03801-3912

Offices and agents throughout the world

The names of the children in this book have been changed to protect their privacy.

Editor: Tom Newkirk
Acquisitions Editor: Scott Mahler
Cover Designer: Barbara Werden

Library of Congress Cataloging-in-Publication Data
Allen, Camille Ann.
    A partnership in literacy : teacher education in an urban school
/ Camille A. Allen.
        p.   cm.
    Includes bibliographical references (p.).
    ISBN 0-435-08859-9
    1. Socially handicapped children—Education—United States—
Language arts—Case studies.   2. Education, Urban—United States—
Case studies.   3. Student teaching—United States—Case studies.
4. English teachers—Training of—United States—Case studies.
5. Sullivan Elementary School (Newport, R.I.)   I. Title.
LC4085.A44   1996
371.96'7—dc20   95-39274
                                                                      CIP

Printed in the United States of America on acid-free paper
99   98   97   96   DA   1   2   3   4   5   6

to FRED
for every reason

Contents

Foreword

A Partnership in Literacy is a fresh, practical look at what schools of education need to do as they enter the twenty-first century. Children, teachers, and schools in cities are isolated from university campuses. If universities were prepared to work with city schools, new partnerships could be established for the mutual learning of each. Sadly, few universities actually encourage their faculties to work with schools beyond the campus. Universities reward publication and on-campus teaching as they should, but seldom recognize the need for faculty members to work with public school teachers along with their own students. Indeed, even if deans encouraged faculty to become involved outside the university, campus expertise does not include skills needed to deal with the rough and tumble of city schools.

Camille Allen, the author of *A Partnership in Literacy*, didn't have that expertise either. Over a five-year period, however, she gradually developed these skills by working side by side with her students, local teachers, and an administrator in a city school where 87 percent of the students are economically and educationally disadvantaged. This book is the story of how and what they learned—including the failures, adjustments, detailed breakthroughs in child literacy learning, and, finally, a broad expansion of a program to involve students from throughout the campus.

Picture Dr. Allen's university reading methods class on a small college campus where most of the students are middle- to upper-class young women in their late teens and twenties. Half the class have just started to work in a city school and speak of their struggles to teach reading and writing. The rest of the students are puzzled over the details of discussions about first-grade children and the struggles of their campus colleagues trying to teach them. Dr. Allen is struck by the inability of the noninvolved students to participate in either the theory or the practical aspects of teaching children. As a result, she makes arrangements so that in the next and succeeding semesters, *all* of her students work and study in the city school.

Dr. Allen leads this project and its subsequent expansions by establishing the notion of partnership as the guiding principle. By exploring and demonstrating her own reading and writing in class, she invites students to read and write with her. Students, in turn, work to discover the power of reading and writing in their own lives.

They share memories, including many of experiences that placed books and writing in a negative light. Dr. Allen also shares her own literacy history through her portfolio. At the same time, they all learn through one-on-one tutoring with the city school's first graders, many of whom do not come from strong, literate traditions. With the students' sudden immersion in actually teaching children, the need for specific details on how to teach takes on new significance. In short, the combination of these efforts reestablishes the function and power of literacy in the college students' lives.

Dr. Allen's emphasis on tutoring for "emergent" professionals is instructive, especially when it involves children who are learning to read and write for the first time. As I read her story, I found myself rethinking the place of tutoring for students learning to teach. I thought of how much advanced teachers learn through Marie Clay's Reading Recovery program. While children make breakthroughs in learning to read in the Recovery program, teachers make professional advances in their teaching. Allen helped me to reconsider tutoring as a student's first contact with teaching.

In my own early days as a preservice teacher, our instructors brought us into the profession through working with small groups of children. They figured an entire class would be too much for us. I taught a short phonics lesson to three children. One got the sound/symbol correspondence; the others didn't. I wondered what was wrong with the other two children. With one-on-one tutoring, however, it is difficult to blame the patient. There are just two people involved—the tutor and the child.

Through four case studies, Camille Allen shows the details of progress for both child and student. We follow the tutor through first preparations, failures, and first success. We read the student's own journal reflections about each lesson and follow the story through to the child's successful reading. We hear the frank language of children: one addresses his tutor, "I'm sick of you and your books." We see that three months later the same child reads from posters and papers on bulletin boards and stops anyone in reach to hear him read his favorite books.

Quite frankly, I was worried about some of the college students' initial views of the children. At first, some pity the children. They seem to say, "How sad; what a tough break for children to live in a place like this." Fortunately, strong personal contact, sound teaching, and guidance change any notion of pity to "these kids are just like any others—now what can we do to teach them?" In the context of the classroom, students acquire the skills to help the children read and write. For this reason, readers will find that the teaching skills developed in this book will apply to all children who are learning to read and write for the first time.

A Partnership in Literacy provides strategies for preparing lessons for the children and supplies the details of materials students who tutor will need. It also includes lists of pattern books with predictable language and suitable books for both read-alouds and specific child interests.

Allen's program is a microcosm of what future teachers need for both professional and personal development. Camille Allen, choosing the medium of tutoring, shows just how students on any campus can learn to teach. In this instance, students learn as much about the culture of the school as they do about reading. They are exposed to the social and pedagogical issues of city schools—the very issues that will confront more and more of us in the twenty-first century. *A Partnership in Literacy* provides a rough map to teacher education, with all the instructional and administrative pitfalls that accompany such an undertaking. Most important, it shows us quite clearly the difference detailed teaching and learning can make in the lives of students and young children.

—Donald H. Graves

Acknowledgments

Writing this book has been an adventure and a learning experience. I have many people to thank.

I thank Don Graves for his tremendous support. He believed I had something to say and taught me how to say it. It has been a privilege to have him as a mentor and a friend.

Thanks to Jane Hansen. She was always so interested in my projects and my writing. She patiently responded to each chapter as the book evolved.

I am particularly grateful to Tom Newkirk, my editor. His straightforward nature and sense of humor made it easier to cut, revise, and polish this manuscript.

For the collaboration and friendship of Michael Segerson, I am much indebted. As principal of Sullivan School he possesses vision, holds high expectations for his students, and remains flexible to accommodate new endeavors that we attempt on a semester basis.

I thank all the teachers at Sullivan School for opening their classrooms to my students for a variety of field and tutoring experiences. In particular I want to thank Emily Carr, Brenda Hawkins, Missy Mellekas, Lorén Spears, and Vicki Vaillancourt for their participation in our initial collaborations, which were not always smooth. Their patience, suggestions, and expertise have strengthened the learning environment for both their children and my students.

I would like to thank the children at Sullivan School. The friendship and challenges they provide develop my students into fine teachers.

My students deserve praise and admiration. I can't thank them enough. Not only do they make a difference in the lives of the children, but their questions, enthusiasm for learning, and ideas challenge me to continue to improve my own teaching and learning. They make my job a pleasure.

I would like to thank the administration and faculty at Salve Regina for their belief in community outreach. This supportive environment fosters a sense of caring among our students and enables them to translate their energies into the service of others.

To the many friends, colleagues, and students who have read and responded to various excerpts of the book, I am grateful. Your time and encouraging words are appreciated.

Thanks to all the people at Heinemann, especially Scott Mahler and Renée Nicholls, for their guidance and encouragement throughout the editing and publishing process.

Thanks too to Nancie Atwell, Don Graves, Jane Hansen, Lucy Calkins, Don Murray, Tom Newkirk, Regie Routman, Mike Rose, and Ralph Fletcher for writing wonderful books. They have altered my teaching. I thank them too for influencing my writing. Many times when I would encounter writer's block, I would reread passages from their books and get charged to continue.

Finally, I am lucky to have Fred, Don, and Beck, my family, who bring love and laughter to the rest of my life.

Chapter One

Join Forces

Toward the end of my fifty-mile commute to the university, I descend from the summit of the Newport Bridge. It arches above Narragansett Bay and spans a two-mile stretch. At the end of the bridge the road divides. The right fork leads to Salve Regina, a private university in a well-to-do neighborhood on the edge of the Atlantic Ocean. I work there as a professor teaching language arts methods courses and preparing preservice teachers.

The left fork leads to Sullivan Elementary School, which abuts the edge of the city's public housing. Between 75 and 80 percent of the school's children are labeled moderate- or high-risk. Before the spring of 1989, I seldom took the left fork, ignoring the plight of schools like Sullivan and never realizing the valuable resources and contributions the classroom teachers and children could make to me and my students. This book is the story about how I took the left fork and how a university and school learned to work together.

National data show that schools and universities need each other . . . but only if universities have learned enough to help the schools. By the year 2000, 50 percent of all urban school children will be from ethnic minority groups (Haberman 1987, 3). Today minority students comprise about 20 percent of the total college population (Evangelauf 1993). However, 47 percent of those minorities enroll in a two- rather than a four-year program (Evangelauf 1993). Compounded by universities' limited visions of essential field experiences for preservice education, a limited pool of future minority preservice teachers will result in a critical shortage of educators who will be willing (much less able) to respond to the needs of America's shifting ethnicity.

Our predominantly white, middle-class college students are not prepared to deal with the realities of teaching in these classrooms. Worse, they do not comprehend the harsh environmental constraints from which these classrooms draw their students. We must begin to

1

mend the schism between America's rich and poor. Students and professors must leave their campuses, work in schools, and learn the language and culture of the cities' teachers and children.

The Right Fork

When I take the right fork from the Newport Bridge, I pass between the two cemeteries that border Farewell Street. I cruise right onto America's Cup Avenue, which is lined with expensive shops and gourmet restaurants. Red and blue flags luff high above the eighty-foot yachts rocking gently in the harbor. Tourist information signs pave the way to the Breakers, Rosecliff, Marble House, and other turn-of-the-century summer cottages of families like the Vanderbilts.

I drive up Memorial Boulevard and stop at the intersection of Spring Street. It gives me the chance to glance at St. Mary's Church, where John Kennedy and Jackie Bouvier were married. The light changes, and I climb up to Bellevue. Mercedes and BMWs slow down to allow morning joggers the chance to keep their pace as they cross Bellevue Avenue and head toward the ocean.

When I reach the black, wrought iron gates of the main entrance to our university, I sometimes see the gardeners mulching the award-winning rose gardens or pruning the towering, hundred-year-old beech trees. I park my car and survey the rolling surf of the Atlantic as it crashes onto First Beach at the end of the Cliff Walk. Some mornings fog horns moan, and the salt air interrupts my thoughts of work. It reminds me of the days when I was young and would build sand castles up and down the shoreline of Rhode Island.

Working at Salve Regina has been my first teaching experience at a private university. I was a product of public school, and all my previous jobs were in the public sector. I remember that during my interview for this job, the Academic Dean asked if I had seen any graffiti around the campus. I thought it was an odd question at the time. I hadn't. She explained that any such antics were treated seriously, and the damage was eradicated by the very next day. I've worked there since 1984, and she was right.

This immaculate, ocean-side atmosphere was only one of the things I had to get used to. There were seldom any portable radios blaring or students hanging from windows yelling to friends to make dinner arrangements. Students would contact me if they were going to be absent and later telephone to see what they had missed.

Over the past ten years I've taught less than a handful of men in my classes. Only one African American and one Asian American have graduated from our education program. Many of the young women in my classes graduated from private secondary schools. They attend classes wearing Ralph Lauren blouses, genuine pearl necklaces, and exuding the latest fragrances from Benetton. Some drive hand-me-down Mercedes that their families have given them or Saabs because they are safe and reliable.

Some of my students, however, struggle for scholarships or loans and work twenty hours a week to be able to return to school for another semester. They work as baby-sitters, waitresses, and bartenders to supplement any financial aid they receive from the university.

Many of my students live on campus in dorms, houses, and converted mansions. Some live in off-campus housing or apartments. Few commute more than five miles.

My students and I are representatives of what Shirley Brice Heath (1983) refers to as the "mainstream" group:

> Mainstreamers exist in societies around the world that rely on formal education systems to prepare children for participation in settings involving literacy. Cross-national descriptions characterize these groups as literate, school-oriented, aspiring to upward mobility through success in formal institutions, and looking beyond the primary networks of family and community for behavioral models and value orientations. (391–2)

Most of my students are impeccably groomed, with manners to match. Although they are accustomed to the luxury that their upbringing has afforded them, it doesn't get in the way of their commitment to community service and volunteerism. If a member of the community calls me with a request, within minutes I can produce a list of volunteers to complete the task. They are caring individuals.

The Left Fork

At the end of the Newport Bridge, when I take the left fork, I head toward Sullivan School. Instead of mansion-lined streets, bungalows crowd the neighborhood. Patches of crabgrass alternate with cracked sidewalks and narrow driveways. Convenience stores, corner restaurants, neighborhood schools, and churches decorate the journey.

My final right leads me to Sullivan, which looks like many of America's single-storied, brick elementary schools constructed in the 1950s. A cement canopy supported by rusty metal arches covers the crumbling sidewalk to the entrance. The main doors, with gray, peeling paint, open to reveal a brick-lined bed of yellow and peach plastic flowers. Windows opposite the entrance display student papers and a royal blue-and-red banner that brags, "SULLIVAN SCHOOL DRUG FREE!"

Classroom doors continuously burst open, allowing adults and children to fulfill daily schedules and chores. A multicolored caterpillar of kindergarten children wiggles its way down a dark hallway into the cafeteria. You know it's the cafeteria because the aroma of steamed green beans overpowers the general fragrance of waxed floors, chalk, and gym sneakers.

The music teacher pushes a cart piled high with a record player and stacks of faded, blue songbooks. He careens to the left to avoid a first grader preoccupied with the importance of carrying the hot-lunch list to the office.

Through casual observance you would think this is a typical day at a typical elementary school. It is a typical day. But it is not the typical elementary school that you would expect to find in the wealthy city of Newport.

Almost all children who attend Sullivan School live in public housing, which includes low-income and enlisted-military subsidized housing. Newport has the largest *per capita* concentration of subsidized housing in Rhode Island. Eighty-seven percent of the students are considered disadvantaged learners.

Most of the teachers who work at Sullivan have been there for years. They work hard, and they enjoy it. They are used to the effects that drugs, divorce, child abuse, and second languages impose upon learning. Over the years my students have worked with children who have witnessed their parents being arrested during the night for drug busts. Other children have suffered sexual molestation in their homes. Crack-addicted mothers have left their children to be cared for by older siblings or in some cases abandoned them completely, leaving them to be brought up by grandmothers. Children nonchalantly discuss with my students the fact that one or both of their parents are in jail.

Rhodes and Brown (1991) have begun to identify the factors that help these children succeed despite the odds. Among the factors that promote invulnerability and resiliency in at-risk children are improved environmental circumstances, good relationships with teachers, and positive school experiences. At-risk children need the love and literacy of role models to support them in their battles against educational and environmental obstacles. They need to build relationships with people who care enough about them and their learning to encourage and press them to achieve their potential. Some of those people are my university students.

Joining Forces

Each fall on Wednesday mornings, the students in my reading and language arts course travel as a cohort to the first-grade classrooms at Sullivan School. They work with the same teachers and children for the entire semester. They develop a sense of community and common experience. They rely on each other, their classroom teachers, and me as they sort out their attitudes; conquer their fears; and become familiar with lifestyles, cultures, and teaching methods that directly contrast with anything they experienced when they went to school. This book describes the learning, change, and growth of both the university students and the Sullivan children. It lets readers eavesdrop on conversations, read student journals, and observe classroom lessons both at the elementary school and at the university. It not only reveals the strengths of the many literacy experiments we have attempted over the past five years, but it also lets readers share in the pitfalls and disappointments. In addition, it explains how our commitment to the potential of the children at Sullivan led us to create a number of outreach courses that afford opportunities for both education and noneducation majors to enhance the literacy of children.

Kenneth Sirotnik (1990) synthesized the advice of a number of prominent researchers and educational philosophers who explored the moral questions they felt had to be asked and answered before meaningful educational reform could take place. He believes that future teachers need to build moral character as well as knowledge. They need to create communities of caring and trust, and they need to engage in reflective practice and collaboration.

Universities and public schools can't achieve these goals if they remain in two separate worlds. They need each other. When the public school is labeled at-risk, the need becomes acute. The ironic part is that universities are at-risk, too. And they are unaware of it. If my students had not joined forces with Sullivan, our teacher education program might have become irrelevant. But more important, we would not have become aware of and concerned enough about the future and literacy of these disadvantaged children to strive to make a difference in their lives.

Our journey has been far from perfect, and we admittedly take turns at bungling, but we set high expectations and strive to meet new challenges. I hope that readers will see themselves in some of our experiences and realize that they too can negotiate possibilities into realities. Let me begin by describing how our partnership began.

Chapter Two

Pilot Project

September 1989

Crisp fall days signal the opening of school. On the first day of my reading methods course I tell my students about the opportunity to tutor some first graders:

> A few of the teachers at Sullivan School are willing to have you work with their children for one hour each week. I don't know the teachers, but I do know they are in transition. They want to move from teaching reading with a basal to using an approach that is more child-centered and developmentally appropriate.

As I discuss this opportunity with my students, I also know that the majority of classroom teachers revere the use of the basal reader and a more traditional approach to the teaching of reading and writing. As I prepare my students for the classrooms at Sullivan where they will be working, I'm torn between what currently is and what I think ought to be a part of my students' preservice education.

Outside my college classroom, the impact of the research of Donald Graves (1983), Jane Hansen (1987), and Nancie Atwell (1987) is beginning to work its way into the fiber of America's schoolrooms. The writing process, whole language, and the concepts of time, choice, and response in relation to reading and writing are beginning to creep into the methods employed by risk-taking teachers. However, my students and I have had little exposure to and experience with these methods and philosophies of teaching language arts as *we* progressed through elementary and secondary school. In fact, in 1988 when I taught the reading and language arts courses for the first time, I only mentioned these approaches. They were more of an afterthought.

From the two sections of my reading course, twenty-five students volunteer to go to Sullivan and join the teachers in their experimentation with some of these new methods. During their first meeting on campus after they work with the children, I ask some of the volunteers to share their initial experiences. One student begins:

> The thirteen of us were introduced to the class. It was then up to us to team up with a student of our choice. I chose a cute little girl named Anita. Our instructions were not very specific; we were there to help the children write in their journals. I talked to Anita for awhile, then I read a Mr. Happy book to her. When we finished, she wrote a little Mr. Happy story of her own. She drew the pictures and told me what sentences to write. During the last fifteen minutes, the whole class sat in a group on the floor. Each student had a chance to read their story aloud and answer questions about it. Everyone was very proud of their work. I'm looking forward to next week.

Throughout the semester, the students' personal anecdotes reveal that they are involved with journal writing, language experience stories, and getting acquainted with some children with troubled home lives.

Because only some of my students are working at Sullivan, during our campus classes I can only allocate a few minutes to discuss their experiences. Often when a Sullivan volunteer describes a troubling situation and asks for advice, members of the class sympathize with her. As I discuss possible alternatives for dealing with her concerns, however, I notice that students who don't work with a child at Sullivan glance at their notebooks, flip through the pages of their texts, or chat quietly together. Some sit staring as if they're waiting for a commercial to be over so they can return to the main show. They want to cover the course content and get ready for the test. They have their own course expectations, and I sense a bit of jealousy on their part as well.

I squeeze in a few visits to Sullivan to observe the interactions among the new partners, and I witness a number of productive exchanges. Although some of my students seem unsure of themselves and engage in more art than reading and writing experiences, the majority do a respectable job of translating theory into practice. They are learning to teach reading and writing through a hands-on approach. It is very unstructured and looks messy. But learning is messy. I watch them build reading and writing lessons around the interests of the children and trust the children to choose their own way to learn. They listen to and prize the children's feelings and opinions.

There is a lot of laughter; broad smiles paint the faces of children who treasure the extra attention. My students' weekly visits generate enthusiasm that motivates the children. I notice that even after the Salve students leave for the day, several children continue to share among themselves the new books they just created with their university buddies.

December 1989

Toward the end of the semester, I collect the journals from my twenty-five volunteers. Their entries trace brief learning histories between pairs of friends who negotiate literacy together. Among Carolyn's entries she writes:

> *9/26*   Gina is not very experienced using words. She tries very hard though. Her journal is funny and shows incredible imagination. She doesn't have any concept of the connection between written words and speech. I guess that's what I'm here to teach her. . . .
>
> *10/24*   . . . Gina surprises me often. Today, I started kidding her about becoming a famous author. She responded with enthusiasm and began copying titles of books displayed before her. She wrote fast and furiously. I was shocked and impressed. She could read the titles back to me.
>
> *11/7*   Today Gina read *The Gingerbread Man* to me with just a few mistakes. I don't understand how she did this when she seems to have problems with sight words such as *the* otherwise. She is better at reading than she is letting on. I'm not sure if she just likes to get extra help or her confusion with certain lessons is genuine.

As I read my students' journals I see many of them struggling, like Carolyn, as they attempt to clarify what they should be doing at Sullivan. I see their growing interest and involvement with children who often entertain them with vivid imaginations and shock them with sporadic increases in their reading and writing ability. My students learn to redirect their energies and lessons to encourage the first-grade children. This is not a simple process for any of them.

On the positive side, I realize that this semester's casual experiment in collaboration taught me the difference between disconnected versus connected learning. Although sometimes unsure and struggling, those who volunteered were at least engrossed in intimate and intense exchanges of language. They read, spoke, listened, and wrote with real children. They built meaningful relationships, fostered a love of reading and learning, and enjoyed themselves in the process. They engaged in complex and significant learning experiences that the rest of us who remained on campus only shared through their occasional anecdotes. We lived vicariously on the boundaries of their learning. These volunteers applied their knowledge about the teaching of reading and writing, took risks, and learned because they were actively involved.

On the negative side, this semester frustrated me because I could only send about half my students to Sullivan. There was a real need to talk, and I couldn't spend enough class time resolving the volunteers' practical concerns. Also, I couldn't coordinate our on-campus course work with their evolving needs. My pre-existing outline for the semester left little room for flexibility. In addition, although I learned the value of having students keep journals, I didn't maximize their use because I waited until the end of the semester to collect them.

Despite the drawbacks of the pilot project, this semester has made me realize that my students and I can no longer remain isolated on campus. I changed my belief that a professor-centered language arts course can serve the needs of future teachers.

February 1990

I make an appointment to visit the principal, Mike Segerson. Mike is not like most principals I remember when I went to school. A trim man in his mid-forties, he has a good sense of humor and is very open with his students. I like that. He's interested in new ideas, holds great hope for his kids, and is flexible. His prematurely gray mustache caps a quick smile. He tells me about his ideas for the fall of 1990:

> I'm going to move all my first-grade teachers together next fall. They'll be on the same corridor, and their classrooms will have adjoining doors. They'll have a common planning time too. That's when they can meet with your students. I think it's important that they have time to share ideas, especially as they struggle with integrating thematic units and moving away from the basal. Here's a copy of their schedules.

We decide that my students will work with the children for an hour and then meet with the teachers for a half hour while the children are out of their classrooms for physical education, music, art, or library.

As I'm leaving, Mike grins and adds:

> And speaking of teachers, we don't know who two of them will be yet. We have one first-grade teacher retiring, so that leaves Vicki Vaillancourt and Missy Mellekas. We need to hire two new teachers. When I hire them, I'm going to make sure that they understand they'll be working with you and your university students and that our common goal is to move from a basal approach to a more child-centered, whole language approach. I'm looking forward to working with you in the fall.

I feel very comfortable talking with Mike. We've had casual conversations before, but this is really the first time we've met to plan for the future of our partnership. It is important for me to listen to him. In order for our collaboration to be successful, I have to understand and balance the needs of both Sullivan and Salve.

Public schools don't have a lot of money. When my twenty-five volunteers bombarded the two first grades during the pilot semester, they constructed books and consumed supplies. I anticipate that I will be bringing between fifty and sixty college students to Sullivan each week in the fall. Multiply that by fifteen weeks and it translates into reams of paper.

Toward the end of the semester, therefore, I write for and receive a grant of $452.94 from my university to purchase supplies for the Sullivan children. With this money, we also purchase the following professional books to share with the teachers and my students:

The Craft of Children's Writing by Judith Newman

Early Detection of Reading Difficulties by Marie Clay

Experiment with Fiction by Donald H. Graves

For the Good of Earth and Sun by Georgia Heard

Insult to Intelligence by Frank Smith

Joining the Literacy Club by Frank Smith

Living and Learning Mathematics by David J Whitin, Heidi Mills, and Timothy O'Keefe

New Policy Guidelines for Reading by Jerome C. Harste

Portraits of Whole Language Classrooms by Heidi Mills and Jean Anne Clyde

Sand and Stones by Marie Clay

Spel is a Four-Letter Word by Richard Genry

Spell by Writing by Wendy Bean and Christine Bouffler

Teaching Drama to Young Children by Mem Fox

Transitions: From Literature to Literacy by Regie Routman

What's Whole In Whole Language by Kenneth S. Goodman

When Writers Read by Jane Hansen

The Whole Language Evaluation Book by Kenneth S. Goodman, Yetta M. Goodman, and Wendy J. Hood

Writing Begins at Home by Marie Clay

Writing: Teachers and Children at Work by Donald H. Graves

I schedule a meeting with the two first-grade teachers, Vicki and Missy, at Sullivan after school and I give the teachers a copy of the new textbook that I plan to use with my students in the fall, *Reading As Communication* (May 1990). We talk for a time about some of the topics I include in my course, and I listen to what they are trying to do in their classrooms. We end by discussing the fact that no one still knows who the other two new first-grade teachers will be. What we do know is that fifty-nine university students have registered for my reading/language arts course and that eighty-six first graders will be waiting at Sullivan to greet us in September.

Chapter Three

Great Expectations

Fall 1990

At Sullivan School, I spot Mike Segerson on morning duty surrounded by hundreds of kids. The fifth graders fuss over the primary-aged children. It's tricky subduing and channeling playground energy into straight lines. The children march into school in front of Mike and me while the administrative assistant bellows at a few late children who nonchalantly skip through the grassy field across the street from the school.

I enter the building and find my university students gathered in the lobby. A short, dark-haired teacher parades his little ones along the corridor and jokingly calls out to my students, "Think twice about it girls, think twice!"

They laugh. His remarks ease the tension. We funnel down the corridor and position ourselves outside the four first-grade classrooms. Some of the little ones on bathroom break line up against the beige-tiled corridor wall. One wiry first-grade boy whispers, "Oh no, more of them. Why do they all have to be girls?"

This fall my students and I will be working with the four first-grade teachers. Vicki Vaillancourt, a slender dark-haired woman in her mid-forties, has been teaching school for twenty years. She's the veteran of the group. Vicki worked in special education for a while and then became a classroom teacher. She worked with the twenty-five volunteers in the pilot project last fall. When I visited her classroom, she displayed love and respect for her children with her mild-mannered voice and calming smile.

The second teacher, Missy Mellekas, has been teaching for about ten years. She used to work at a private school and has now transferred her energies into public school education. I also met this petite woman last year when I visited her first-grade class. She shared with me some learning centers she created from her work in a graduate course. She darted from place to place, ran her hands through her dark hair, and smiled broadly. Her high-spirited nature ensured that there would never be a lull in her daily routine.

Today I will meet Emily Carr and Lorén Spears, the other two first-grade teachers, for the first time. They were hired right before school opened. Emily studied and worked in the area of early childhood education. Lorén, a Native American, completed her student teaching and then helped with the education of members of her tribe. For both teachers, this is their first experience at the first-grade level and at teaching in an at-risk elementary school. This is also Lorén's first full-time job.

I follow one group of my students into Emily's room. Blonde and in her forties, this woman introduces us with exuberance, "Boys and girls, look who's come to visit us. It's the Salve Buddies!" She randomly matches each of her students with mine as they enter the classroom. Some of my students have one elementary child, several have two. As the last student enters the room there are three elementary children left—she inherits all three. The students in the other rooms are also matched with partners.

During the morning, I wander among the four first-grade classrooms. They teem with new sets of wiggling, talking, and laughing buddies. Shoe boxes labeled with children's names hold books they have constructed. Desks cluster in pods rather than isolated rows. Writing tools fill jars; pencils, scissors, and staplers have been placed within easy access of tiny fingers. Crates of children's literature books fill nooks and crannies around the edges of the rooms. Photos of each child decorate bulletin boards. Dictated sentences and wall stories circumvent the science corner, which has pine cones, bugs, magnifying glasses, and styrofoam cups with seedlings. I duck under a string that acts as a clothesline for many of the children's art projects.

Our first hour together flies by. Lorén, a tall young woman with a braid, turns off the lights to signal that it's time for a transition. She flashes a bright smile and confidently commands her children to prepare for physical education. Reluctantly, my students extricate themselves from the first graders' loving grasps and nonstop questions, clean up their respective messes, and coax the children to line up in the corridor. A few of the children wave to their new friends.

The other three first-grade teachers and the university students from their classrooms join us in Lorén's room. Mike Segerson, the principal, arrives to welcome the class. When everyone is settled, I introduce him. Mike stands and addresses my students:

> Hi and welcome. I'd like to start out by telling you a little bit about the school. We have 326 students here at Sullivan. We have thirty-five teachers on staff, one kindergarten, two pre-one classes, four

first grades, four second grades, three thirds, three fourths, three fifths, and one special education class for children with behavior disorders. To let you know a little about these kids, not one in the school has parents who own their own house. They come from Parkholm, Tonomy Hill, Rolling Green, Festival Field and Bayside Village. Some live in the Bridgeview Condominiums or navy-enlisted housing.

Last year we took a group to the fire station, and for some it was the first time they had gone beyond their neighborhood. When we took a group to a farm, we had to cross the Newport Bridge. Fifty percent of them had never seen a bridge. They get no reading at home—none. They don't have books or magazines in their homes. They have parents who care but are scared to come in here.

I've had kids bring bullets in and put them on my desk. Sometimes they bring in crack vials that they find in the street. We provide a safe, secure environment. Some of these kids are stressed out. They love you and they need you. I ask that once you get paired up, if you are sick or your car breaks down, call in. I've seen a child who sat in the corner and refused to interact because his buddy didn't show up. They understand if you are sick, and they can accept that. But they get angry. They are disappointed and they act up. They do it to substitute teachers all the time.

Another thing, you are professionals now. There are going to be times when the kids are going to tell you things, things you didn't want to know. When you go back to the dorms or your apartments, don't discuss these kids and things that they tell you. If there are times when you just feel you have to talk about this, talk to Dr. Allen or your classroom teachers, but don't spread it in public. You are a professional.

If there is anything you need me to do, if you have questions, if you need supplies, just let me know—or let Dr. Allen know, and she's sure to let me know.

As Mike speaks, my students stare, frozen with anticipation. New endeavors hold all players hostage to great expectations and fears. I know what they're thinking today because I have been corresponding with them through their journals. Recently, one student wrote:

> 9/11   . . . I feel very excited but also very nervous about teaching. I guess it is only normal though. It seems that there are so many strategies (dos and don'ts) that have to be thought about when you teach. . . . Right now it just seems as if everything is being thrown at us at once.

I know I'm placing a strain on them by sending them into the classroom with little preparation. But they aren't the only anxious ones. As Mike speaks, my mind darts in all directions. I remember a conversation I shared with a colleague at the university a few months ago. I was excited about the success of last fall's pilot project and the plans we arranged for this semester. I explained, "I'm thinking about putting them out there right away. They barely will have cracked their texts and they'll be applying their knowledge or lack of."

"Well, that's where we differ philosophically," she responded. "I feel they need a strong foundation in the concepts and methods before they apply them. They have to know what they are doing before we put them into the schools."

"I don't know," I said. "It seems that it's only in the field of teaching that we talk about it for so long before we dig in. When we try to learn anything else, like skiing or playing piano, we practice right away. We make mistakes, and we get better."

"Yes, but in those areas you are learning for yourself," she argued. There is no one else affected. Here you are talking about elementary children. Our students are practicing with someone else's learning."

She made her point.

I made my decision. We'd go into Sullivan right away.

When we finish our first visit to Sullivan I read my students' journals:

> 9/12   The things that shocked me the most are the neighborhoods, houses, families, and areas that the children come from. I have never been opened up to children that have seen drugs and do not come from a two parent family environment. Hearing the stories did make me feel a little anxious. It may be difficult to relate to their problems, especially in the beginning. We must all leave the university at one point and look around. Life is beautiful here, but down the street it's tough.

They also have difficulty accepting the fact that some of the children can't read and write at all. In fact, some children have no concept of what a story is. They've rarely (if ever) been read to, and their experiential background is limited to what they see on television and in their immediate neighborhood. Another student comments in her journal:

> Sullivan School was not what I expected. Where I am from the students at that age already know how to read or are almost at that stage. When the students don't have an idea about words, letters, or such it surprises me but probably just because of the background that I have had.

One student's comments reflect how most of us were feeling:

> Today I was really nervous and as the day progressed I became more nervous. I felt like I was watching everyone else in the classroom instead of paying attention to myself and my student. I thought,

"Am I doing this right?" and "What am I actually supposed to be doing?" . . . I think I was just shocked to finally be in the classroom.

We all wonder where we will go from here.

The four first-grade teachers are not experts. They are in the process of change, struggling to familiarize themselves with the latest techniques and trying to use trade books to teach reading and writing. They are forfeiting their planning time each Wednesday to accommodate hordes of university students who have the potential to raise havoc in their classrooms. In addition, Emily and Lorén have to adapt to a new environment and teaching at a new grade level. The pressure of my students' inquiring minds and eyes can't make it easy for them.

My students are not experts. For many, it's the first time they've entered an elementary classroom in fifteen years. For some, the memories of how they learned to read and write conflict with the whole language and writing process philosophy we are all experimenting with. In addition, they didn't attend schools like Sullivan.

And I certainly am no expert. I've never coordinated such a large-scale on-campus/off-campus project in which I have to meet the needs and interests of so many and at the same time ensure that everyone learns something in the process. I don't want to set up a hierarchy of authority in which everyone believes that my knowledge is superior or more useful than theirs. I know I don't have all the answers.

According to Mike Rose, author of *Lives on the Boundary* (1989), the best course for my students to take is to roll up their sleeves and plunge in. He compares his students' experiences with those of

> a traveler in a foreign land [who] best learns names of people and places, how to express ideas, ways to carry on a conversation by moving around in the culture, participating as fully as he can, making mistakes, saying things half right, blushing, then being encouraged by a friendly native speaker to try again. He'll pick up the details of grammar and usage as he goes along. What he must not do is hold back from the teeming flow of life, must not sit in his hotel room and drill himself on all possible gaffes before entering the streets. He'd never leave the room. (142)

My students and I are about to immerse ourselves in the teeming flow of elementary school life, gaffes and all. We'll experiment together.

Chapter Four

Chaotic False Starts

And experiment we do. How well I remember that first day at Sullivan School and the many Wednesday mornings since. Some prove successful; others disastrous. But we learn from each one. Before I describe our current program, let me share some of our first experiences.

My Students Work with the Children

When we first begin our collaboration with Sullivan School, I advise my students to talk with the children, find out what interests them, and become acquainted. I tell them to read to the children and have the children dictate some language experience stories. Because each child and each situation will be different, I decide to leave the weekly planning to my students.

It is difficult to keep track of fifty-nine university students and eighty-six first graders. Each week after their visit to Sullivan, my students write and submit to me a summary of how things went. They also include questions, which I compile and try to address during our next on-campus classes. To develop their lessons, they also spend time sharing ideas back at their dorms. Some even telephone their parents who are teachers or principals. As a result, some of my students successfully translate theory into practice. But there are a good number who don't. They can't decide what their children need. They fail to plan, or plan inappropriate activities. They seem lost week after week.

Determining appropriate teaching strategies takes experience and the skill to systematically observe children. Some of my students have neither. For all of our successes each week, there seem to be as many or more difficult situations that arise. My students often write "HELP!" in their journals—and with good reason. Sometimes they overestimate their children's abilities only to find that the children lack the background knowledge to complete the lessons they've planned. Sometimes they underestimate the children's capabilities and the children become bored or finish the lesson within a few minutes. At those times, my students are forced to improvise, and they are not experienced enough to do so.

When the classroom teachers see some of my students floundering, they try to help. One time, besides offering suggestions, Missy plans a whole-class lesson for my students to teach. They are to help the children complete a sequencing exercise for *The Little Red Hen.* I can see relief on some of my student's faces. Because of Missy, they have a plan and some direction. Others look disappointed. One in particular tells me she has spent hours preparing a lesson on *The Very Hungry Caterpillar,* and she is frustrated because she has no time to execute it.

During one visit, a child levels with one of my students, "I don't like you, I'm not going to do any work, and I don't like reading stories." My student is heartbroken. She is not alone. Some weeks children sulk, turn their backs to my students, get up, and walk away. If my students are responsible for two children, they are left trying to balance the needs of the remaining child with the attitude of the deserter.

Some of my students spend a series of frustrating Wednesday mornings before breakthroughs occur. For others, real breakthroughs never occur. One student writes in her journal:

> *10/3*   Today was very frustrating for me because Sid and Abby were tired and Abby was also bored. Sid and Henry can read a little but Abby can't and she only adds fuel to the fire by being lazy. She never wants to do what we're doing!!! (What happens to teachers who dislike students? Do they burn in teacher hell?)

By November, many of my students have sharpened their teaching abilities, gained confidence, and reduced their fears of failure. They appear to be ready for a new challenge. I require each of them to design and teach a small-group lesson based on a children's literature book of their choice. Within each first-grade classroom, I divide my students and their accompanying children into four teams. Every week, one member of each of the four teams teaches, while the other students and children in their team participate in the lesson. In this way, my students who are not teaching get to observe their peers teach and also help with behavior management within the group.

Every Wednesday morning for a month, four concurrent literature lessons are taught in each classroom. Sarah, for example, sits in Emily's rocking chair and reads *Ira Sleeps Over* to three first graders and their Salve Buddies. They stare, mesmerized by the tone of her voice and the animation of her expressions. Sarah is surrounded by a sleeping bag and some teddy bears. One of the small boys sits cross-legged and sucks his thumb. A success.

Across the room, Anne Marie leans against the edge of a student's desk. Her audience of nine children and three Salve students sprawls out before her in a semi-circle. The group is unruly, and Anne Marie's valiant attempts to interest the children in *The Polar Express* go awry.

Anne Marie isn't the only one in trouble. Pockets of commotion and chaos erupt in all the first grades. Some of my students don't appear confident in their abilities to teach before their peers or in their selection of books or materials. Although there are some excellent lessons and many of the children exude enthusiasm, others roll restlessly on the floor or refuse to participate. The children are not used to working in a group situation in which they have to share their Salve Buddy with others. Many disrupt the groups in hopes of regaining the total attention of their buddy. In the meantime, the buddies are desperately trying to teach successful lessons in a very noisy, disruptive environment. One student writes in her journal:

> . . . I felt very lost today, I had no control at all. Mrs. Vaillancourt said I should be firm with them and tell them "this is what we are doing today" and they will do it. How do you get them to do what you want without being mean to them (or crying)? I just lost it today and I think they knew they had me. I didn't cry in front of them but it was hard to hold it in. I did after they left. Mrs. Vaillancourt said not to get too upset because she has those days at least once a week.

I don't interrupt these failing lessons because I feel it is important for the students to experience the whole process. Some regain their composure and manage to switch to other activities that eventually bring the children into line. But it isn't ideal. In fact it is almost fatal—and I feel guilty for placing the children and my students in a situation where they are forced to teach and learn a lesson among chaos.

My Students Work with the Teachers

Each week after my students finish teaching individual students or small-group lessons, they congregate with the teachers and me in one large or several small groups to reflect upon theory and methodologies. The function of these large-group sessions changes weekly.

I am aware of the pressure that our invasion places upon the classroom teachers, particularly the new ones. It must not be easy for them to be thrust into the responsibility of guiding preservice teachers when they only are used to working with primary-aged children.

I suggest rather than request that if any of the first-grade teachers would like to demonstrate or discuss any of her classroom procedures or ideas before the whole group, she should feel free to do so. Missy volunteers. She forges to the front of the class, carrying the big book *Boss for a Week*. She explains the purpose of big books and then involves my students in a lesson.

"As I read through this," she begins, "I want you to think about what concepts and skills you might teach."

Missy reads a few pages of the story and embellishes the text with expressive body language. One of my students raises her hand and guesses, "Days of the week?"

"What else, within the language itself?" Missy asks. "Listen. 'Little Caroline, sweet Caroline, hungry, starving, darling, Caroline . . .'"

"Adjectives?"

"Good. I'd do a whole activity on adjectives. How would you describe yourself? Also they'd all love to be Boss. I would create an activity that asks them, 'What would you do if you were boss?' or 'What would you do if you were the teacher?'"

She places a new book on the easel and continues her demonstration. I am happy that Missy volunteered. She not only has instructed my students in appropriate types of learning experiences to implement with the first graders, but she also has affirmed her new position as guide and mentor for large numbers of university students. I can see her confidence growing.

Sometimes during our large-group meetings guest speakers address us. On one occasion, the children's librarian from the local public library shares information about resources available to teachers for planning units. Both the classroom teachers and my students seem impressed with her knowledge and with the number of books available for long-term loan to classrooms.

Another fall morning, a representative from the State Department of Education discusses the fact that when we teach young children we should strive to develop knowledge, skills, dispositions, and feelings. Too often we concentrate on knowledge and skills that require repetition, drill, and practice—the very things that kill or deaden dispositions to learn and the feelings of self-confidence necessary to learn.

She explains that dispositions are habits of the mind, tendencies to react to particular experiences in certain kinds of ways. "You can't teach dispositions, creativity, or interest but you can set the conditions for that to happen," she says. Most of my students haven't learned yet how to balance the development of skills with the development of dispositions. Some spend too much time teaching prepared lessons and drilling the children, while other spend too much time socializing and building self-confidence.

At other times during our group meetings, we watch instructional videos. We enjoy *The Writing Workshop: A World of Difference* by Lucy Calkins and *The Writing and Reading Process* by Jane Hansen and Donald Graves. In these videos, the instructors discuss supportive classroom environments and effective conferencing skills employed by teachers in process classrooms. Sharing the videos at Sullivan gives the classroom teachers, my students, and me a brief chance to discuss our discoveries and insights. Unfortunately, it doesn't allow us enough additional time to fully digest the material and consider ways to implement the lessons in our classes.

At the end of several whole-group sessions, I distribute handouts that I think might benefit my students and the teachers. They deal with tips and techniques teachers might find helpful when working in whole language classrooms. I also introduce some professional books that I have purchased with the grant money from the university. Several of the classroom teachers and my students borrow them.

In response to requests from the classroom teachers and my students, sometimes the four first-grade teachers meet with their respective groups of university students to discuss the progress of their first graders. I join a meeting held by Missy and my students. One is reporting about her child:

> I have Billy. He can use a dictionary and sound out words like that [snaps her fingers]. When spelling, he forgets the final letters. He knows the sounds /sh/ /th/ and /ch/. He doesn't know the proper usage of upper- and lowercase letters. He squeezes all the letters together into one big word. He knows to use a period at the end of a sentence. He doesn't have a problem reading or sounding out any word he comes to. He has a good attitude toward reading, follows directions very well and is shy and keeps to himself. He hesitates to raise his hand even if he knows the answer. He has good listening skills. He knows the structure and organization of a book and can easily count to ten.

Missy asks about Billy's writing skills. The student replies:

> He knows he needs a noun and a verb in a sentence. He wrote a sentence and I said, "Does that look right?" and he said, "No I forgot the action verb!" I was surprised. He loves to read but when it comes to writing he says, "I have to think about what I want to write first" and it takes him about five minutes just to think. Then he's OK. I tried some brainstorming techniques using puppets. It took some time but then he wrote.

These sessions provide extra information for both the classroom teachers and my students. This helps us all to meet the needs of the children. They also show my students the range of abilities in one first-grade classroom. In addition, they help to build trust and rapport between the teachers and my students. My students learn the language of the profession. The teachers treat my students with respect and value their opinions. Often during these meetings, the teachers update my students on what the children have done during the week, discuss resources in their rooms, and express gratitude for the university students' efforts.

Toward the end of the semester, my students and the classroom teachers review the results of their attempts to teach the small-group literature lesson. One of my students, Laura, reports her disaster:

> I really wanted to work with Tomie dePaola's book *Strega Nona* because I loved that book as a child. I even went to see Dr. Allen last week to discuss different types of questions I could ask and how I could construct manipulatives to keep the children involved. We talked about how I should incorporate reading, writing, and predicting in my lesson.
>
> I planned to read the book and have the students re-write the story by acting it out with the puppets I made of the main characters. If all had gone as planned, there should have been six students and one puppet for each. Three were absent, including two Salve Buddies. This made re-telling the story chaotic because there were more puppets than students and everyone was more interested in how many puppets they had instead of thinking about re-telling the story. The kids were OK while I was reading the book but after that they didn't want to participate. When it came time to re-write the story it was like pulling teeth. They lost interest.
>
> I feel so bad. I worked so hard. I guess I did learn something. No matter how prepared you think you are, be prepared for something to go wrong and be ready to deal with it. If you want to teach, you have to learn to think on your feet and be flexible.

During these sessions, my students and their classroom teachers listen, interject positive comments, and offer suggestions. Some of my students borrow ideas for lessons they might try in the future. Those who have observed a modest peer teaching brag about her good ideas and instruction. They also offer positive criticism to their classmates if they note weak areas. They couch their language and are careful to respect each others' vulnerability. They listen to each other and to themselves. It is a time of catharsis and celebration.

Although these sessions are among the most valuable for my students, having university students present small-group lessons to first graders trying to learn to read and write is not the most valuable experience for the children. The noise created by four concurrent lessons in one classroom, coupled with having a different student teacher for each new, nonsequential lesson, is too much for most of the children. I will not repeat this assignment again.

Special Celebrations

Halloween

On many occasions during the first several years of our collaboration, we celebrate together. One such day is our first Halloween.

Little Webster has crimson-red greasepaint smeared all over his round face. Thick jet-black circles outline his brown eyes, and white lipstick smothers his mouth. Brown rubber horns protrude from his forehead. He sports a tomato-red sweatshirt and cape.

"Webster, how do you keep those horns on?" I ask. "I don't see any elastics or headbands or anything."

"Oh, easy," he boasts. "My Mom glued 'em to my head this morning." Kids crowd around him to test the glue's tensile strength.

A clown with a violet wig, bulbous red nose, striped satin jumpsuit, and shoes that slap the pavement carries a wicker basket containing shiny, orange gourds for the children in Missy's class. Minnie Mouse, harlequins, cats, ducks, and farmers parade through the halls on their way to the first-grade wing. The Salve Buddies really have outdone themselves. I have trouble recognizing some of them.

"Happy Halloween," says one of my students as she stands before the group. "Today we have a special Halloween book that we'd like to perform for you. When we are all through you can clap if you like it."

Sitting in Emily's wooden rocking chair, one of my students opens her book and begins to read. As she narrates, the Salve Buddies interpret the adventure using props and pantomime. A Ninja Turtle, a rotund ballerina, the Count Dracula, and children bedecked in homemade costumes stare mesmerized by the action of the conflict. Even Vicki, wrapped in a pale pink lace gown and gold tiara left over from her high school prom, watches with anticipation.

The narrator continues, "'BOO!' shouts Georgie."

The startled children jump, then squeal with laughter. The book ends happily. The children applaud and the Salve Buddies troop to the next class to carry out another performance. In one of the first grades, some of my students join the children in their music class. The record player blares and the room rocks with rhythm and motion. A small witch joins hands with a cat and wiggles to the beat. Two Salve Buddies rock and roll in unison at the edge of the class. They laugh hysterically at their tall friend Sarah as she sways with little Nellie, a child with the smile of Diana Ross and the moves of Paula Abdul.

I pull away from the frenzied festivities and enter Missy's room. She is absent today. There among the costumed brigade cowers a stunned substitute teacher whom I never do meet. Across the room, groups of my students practice with their kids for the upcoming play, an end-of-the-semester performance we decided would be fun to hold for the parents. Ghosts, goblins, and princesses choral read their version of *The Noisy Barnyard*. Seated in a semi-circle and led by Salve clowns and mice, the children recite their lines as they clap their hands to the rhyme of the phrases. The fact that they are dressed in costume exaggerates their usual shenanigans.

Today we leave Sullivan to the relief of the teachers and disappointment of the children. Despite the wild rumpus, spending a day in costume and song has drawn us closer together and has provided novel situations for my students to observe their children and themselves. Some noticed how their children displayed unusual self-confidence with their peers when they worked in a group. In the spirit of the festivities, one child gained the courage to read a big book to her Salve Buddy for the first time. Some Salve students used the opportunity to have their children retell the story the Salve students performed for them earlier; others constructed language experience stories about Halloween.

One of my students sensed the delicate balance between celebration and chaos. Although this day overwhelmed her, she looked at her Sullivan experience in a different light:

10/31   What a day it WAS! The students were off the wall, Mrs. M. was not there and there was no control. I just couldn't wait to get out of there!! . . . Today did have a positive side though. . . . It made me realize that if I student teach in a school like that I could teach ANYWHERE! Is there any way I could request to student teach [as a senior] in a school such as Sullivan? I think it really would be a good experience for me.

The Play

The play takes place in November. That morning, my students arrive at Sullivan by 8:30, lugging boxes and bags filled with pink pig noses, cow horns on headbands, aprons, brooms, carpenter's belts, burlap sacks, American flags, winter hats, posters announcing the months of the year, and a plethora of indescribable yet valued paraphernalia. They dress and decorate their Sullivan Buddies and rehearse their lines for the final time.

In the meantime, the audience trickles into the auditorium between 9:00 and 9:15. Some push strollers, some carry cameras, and some tote babies under their arms. As 9:30 approaches, the four first-grade classrooms empty and the procession of characters enters the auditorium. Mike Segerson greets the parents and introduces Emily Carr's room first.

Emily's children and their Salve Buddies climb the stairs that lead to the stage. Emily motions to them, and they chorus, "A Book of Months by Maurice Sendak." She turns on the tape recorder from behind the musty, faded curtain, and a muffled musical rendition of the book strains from backstage. The big and small participants carry signs that designate the months of the year. Their costumes reflect the seasons. Some wear scarfs and winter coats, some carry posters of spring flowers, and some clutch flags for the Fourth of July. They display their props with pride. During the chorus, confidence surges from their throats and most screech at the top of their lungs, "I told you once, I told you twice, sipping chicken soup with rice!!" In between choruses, they falter, giggle, and try to stay with the program. The other classes follow.

Treat time follows the performances. Costumed children race to the dessert tables and gobble their way to sugar highs. A pensive first grader grabs two brownies, three M&M cookies, and a handful of round cookies sprinkled with powdered sugar. He sits with his Salve Buddy.

A tall man in a military uniform stands with his first-grade daughter and her Salve Buddy. I can't hear what they are saying, but they laugh as the little girl shares her attention between the two grown-ups. She showers them with hugs.

A short African American woman, who bounces incessantly from foot to foot, punctuates her nonstop story with a brilliant smile. Her intonation and mannerisms make it easy to guess that she is Iris's mother. My student listens and wedges in a "Right, right" whenever there is a pause.

Meeting some of the parents reinforces my students' beliefs in themselves as teachers. One of my students writes:

11/14   Today's play was a great experience for all involved. I was so proud and excited. They all were so cute. Meeting Virgil's mom was nice too. I was just thrilled she came. She told me she doesn't read much because she isn't good at it. She also told me she has noticed a great change in Virgil's attitude toward school. He doesn't mind going, so that made me happy. I almost died when she told me Virgil calls me his "Salve babe" at home.

The Class Trip

Toward the end of the semester, we arrange for the children to visit us at Salve Regina. The yellow school buses pull up next to one of Salve's academic buildings, the doors open, and the children pour out. Salve Buddies join hands with the children and usher them into the building. The children barrage their Salve tour guides with questions and comments. "Where do you keep your coats?" "How come you don't have any decorations in your classes?" "Where's your locker?" "This is the biggest building I've ever been in." "My mom goes to college, so I know about college."

They weave their way among the rows of computers in the computer lab. The college students at their work stations pause to smile at the wide-eyed first graders. The kids hike up the circular staircase to the second floor. We crowd into a classroom, and I pop a tape of their play into the VCR. They smirk, giggle, and point as they see themselves in costume singing and acting.

Next we head to the library. Small groups of students eagerly fan out to the reference room while others visit the curriculum resource center. My students read stories and explain how to check out books.

The group has to be in and out of the dining hall before 11:00 A.M., when the college students come in for lunch. Since we have much to see before then, I try to rally the troops. "Pass the word," I say. "We're heading to Ochre Court."

Ochre Court is a turn-of-the-century Newport mansion that sits on the edge of a sprawling, manicured lawn overlooking the Atlantic. It houses the registrar, admissions, and offices of deans and the president. When we arrive, the receptionist who sits near the entrance to the grand hall smiles weakly, unsure if she should call security. I have telephoned several days ahead to warn them of our upcoming visit, but I can tell by her expression that she hasn't been privy to that information.

"We're here on a field trip from Sullivan Elementary School," I explain as the mass of wriggling bodies begins to encroach upon her territory. With obvious reservations, she lets us through.

As soon as I signal the go-ahead, a small group of buddies walk down the center of the grand hall. When they reach the end of the hall, the children press their noses against the plate glass to watch the breakers roll toward the shore. They smudge sparkling glass with their fingerprints, perhaps for posterity.

With an OK from me, it takes only seconds for about half our group to dash up a marble staircase carpeted with thick red rugs. "Look, naked ladies," a small voice shouts. Those of us still on the first floor look up and see a tiny hand pointing to the oil-painted ceilings. It's a clear shot from the marbled floor to the ceiling forty-feet above us, so "naked ladies" ricochets nicely. Emily looks at me and we grin. Above and around us, children inhale the luxury of crystal chandeliers, hand-carved mahogany paneling, imported marble fireplaces, and eighteenth-century paintings.

For what seems an eternity, they run in and out of control. Adult eyes peek from behind office doors. Even the university president takes a moment to see what is happening.

Eventually we manage to corral their energy, bring them safely to the exit, and lead them on to treats in the cafeteria. The cafeteria employees designate a section of the room for us. The college students have baked and delivered their goodies before the group arrived. The dining services donate the milk. The children are fascinated with the milk machine. As the milk climbs the sides of a small child's glass, her eyes open wider and wider.

Several of my students read stories to the children while others pass trays of sweets. Sticky fingers and milk mustaches round out a morning of exploration and laughter.

I watch my students transfuse a bit of their culture to the children. They are so excited to share their university. I overhear them discussing how great and important it is to go to college. They want so much for the children to be able to attain what they so casually have accepted as their right—a good education. This day reminds my students of how fortunate they are.

The yellow school buses pull up in front of the cafeteria and the children line up once again. One of my students picks up her buddy. The child presses her pudgy little face against her big buddy's and kisses her good-bye. They hug and hug and hug.

One by one the children fill the seats of the bus. In ten minutes they will cross town from the world of academia to their own neighborhoods. They rush to one side of the bus to wave farewell. Each window frames a small face.

Chapter Five

Watch, Listen, and Delight

Fall 1994

In *The Art of Teaching Writing* (1994), Lucy Calkins describes how she has learned the real metaphor for literacy learning:

> If we adults listen and watch closely, our children will invite us to share *their* worlds and *their* ways of living in the world. And then, when children become our teachers, showing us what they see and delight in and wonder about and reach toward, then, will we be able to extend what they know and enrich their ways of knowing. Wise teaching . . . begins with watching and listening and delighting in the learner. (53–54)

Watch, listen, and delight in the learner. Let our students become our teachers. This lesson was long in coming but for me, one around which I now design my reading course.

In the past, I imposed my agenda upon my students—and they in turn imposed theirs upon the Sullivan children. I thought field experience should give my students the chance to experiment and try new techniques. Some of the techniques benefitted the children but many didn't. When I reflect, I can't believe all that we crammed into fifteen Wednesday mornings. The pace was frenetic. The spirit fantastic. But it was also amazing that any of us could focus long enough to learn anything. Although each of our activities had merit in itself, in concert they didn't accomplish what a school/university literacy partnership should. I have since realized that cute activities, small-group lessons, guest speakers, and play productions absorbed precious time that could have been better spent understanding and meeting the literacy needs of the Sullivan children.

I no longer view my students' time with the children as an opportunity to "try out" random teaching methods. Instead, it is an invitation to share the children's world and their way of looking at the world. I want my students not only to become a part of the Sullivan School community, but also to become sensitized to the wonder, complexity, and struggles of the children as they experiment with the language arts.

One of my goals for this semester is to help my students become aware of the factors surrounding the lives of children considered at-risk. I also want to help them decide for themselves whether or not the methods employed in whole language and process classrooms are ones they find effective. As a result of their work this semester, they should also be able to clarify the philosophies and methodologies they will adopt for their future classrooms, and to gain the confidence to implement their decisions.

To help my students successfully reach these goals I must listen to, observe, and respond to them. Likewise, to help the children succeed, my students must listen to, observe, and respond to them.

Our Communication System

In her book *When Writers Read* (1987), Jane Hansen speaks of the growing role of the elementary teacher as a person who respects and responds to children, views them as decision makers, charges them with responsibility for their own learning, and learns from them. I have learned that it is impossible to instill this role in my students if I continue to run a teacher-centered classroom at the university.

To transfer decision making and responsibility to my students, and to observe "what they see and delight in and wonder about and reach toward" (Calkins 1994) I've developed a systematic way to listen to, learn from, and respond to each of them twice a week. When I meet my students this semester, I'll give each of them a manila folder with their names and a number written on them. (The numbers will help to keep them in alphabetical order.) I'll give them three sheets of colored paper to use as dividers. I'll ask them to label the sheets *Class Reactions, Reading Reactions,* and *Sullivan Reports.*

Class Reactions

The first section of their manila folders, Class Reactions, will contain their journal writes. During the last five minutes of my classes each day, I'll have them write a brief account of what they learned. I expect that for each of them it will be something different. They can also include questions about what we discussed in class or anything else that might be troubling them. They'll date their entries in the left margin and leave all these communications in their folders throughout the semester. Toby Fulwiler (1991) encourages teachers to have their students end class with this sort of journal write. He explains that although

> issues can be handled orally . . . writing loose thoughts onto paper often generates tighter thinking . . . private writing in a noisy, busy public forum allows the learner to collect thoughts otherwise lost in the push-and-shove hurry to leave class. (205)

Each semester, my students and I pack our university classes with information. Ideas and questions generate and regenerate up to the last second. Slowing the pace to write during the last several minutes of class will allow them to rethink and summarize what they have learned. They'll become accustomed to using writing as a process to clarify their thinking. It will also act as a means to help them determine what they know and what they don't know. Their journal writing will also tune me in to individual or group misunderstandings that I can use as a basis for discussion in upcoming classes.

I've found in the past that when my students write class reactions, they don't just restate my ideas but construct knowledge from their own. In all their journal writing I do not correct or penalize them for errors in grammar, usage, or spelling. We strictly emphasize communication.

Reading Reactions

The second part of their folders, Reading Reactions, will be dedicated to their response to assigned readings from their text or from handouts I will distribute. I designed this section on a modification of Nancie Atwell's (1987) dialogue journals. As she puts it:

> my comments do three things to affirm, challenge, or extend the reader's thinking. These comments take various forms: gossip, questions, recommendations, jokes, restatements, arguments, suggestions, anecdotes, instruction, and "nudges." (275)

My students must read and react to assignments prior to class. This will allow everyone to gather some common background knowledge and allow them to raise better questions. Some students might choose to summarize key points and relate their newfound knowledge to their field experiences at Sullivan. Some might jot down questions that they have while reading or write about ideas that strike them as improbable. Others might relate information to their past reading and writing experiences and, in the process, review the inadequacies of their own schooling.

I will read their written reactions after class. If their responses show that they have misunderstood the material, this will give me the chance to clear up misconceptions in the following class. Because comprehension depends not so much upon what we get from the text but upon the interaction of the text with background knowledge or schema (Durkin 1981; Pearson 1979), each student's experiences will shape a very different analysis and critique of the reading. This should fuel lively classroom discussions.

Sullivan Reports

I designate the third part of their folders for their Sullivan Reports. This will be the most structured part of our weekly communication and will allow me the opportunity to check and reaffirm my students' lesson plans.

Every Friday my students must submit a rough Sullivan plan describing what they will try to accomplish with the children the following Wednesday. I'll take these home over the weekend, make suggestions, jot questions, and return them on Monday morning. This will leave my students two days to revise and finalize their plans.

After my students complete their sessions with the children on Wednesdays, they must submit a summary Sullivan Report. This will restate what they had planned to accomplish; describe how the lesson went; and, based upon these results, what they plan to teach the following week. They will also be responsible for keeping a list of all the books and authors they read to and with the children, as well as a list of all the books the children write. I'll give them the following format as a guide:

SULLIVAN REPORT FORMAT

SULLIVAN VISIT # _____

1. PLAN FOR THE DAY. (This should be an outline of all the activities you have planned for the visit. It is a good idea to break the visit into at least three or four segments. Briefly note why you chose each activity. Examples of possible activities:

Reading
> Read a new book to the child (note title, author).
> Reread a book from last week (note title, author).
> Let the child read to you.
> Choral read together.
> Echo read (you read a sentence and the child repeats it).
> Reread a book the child has written or dictated (note title).

Writing
   Let the child write in her journal.
   Write as the child dictates a story (one sentence per page).
   Let the child write a story (one sentence per page and then illustrate).
   Let the child write the words he knows.
   Let the child keep track of the words she knows in her dictionary.
   Write word cards from stories, let the child copy words.
   Create a portable word wall.

Skill/Strategy Lesson (should be tied to the reading and writing you do with the child that day)
   Sight Words.
   Alphabet Knowledge.
   Phonics Lesson.
   Four Cues.

Games or Children's Choices
   Go Fish.
   Concentration.
   Word Bingo.
   Child's Choice.

2. SUMMARY OF DAY. Here you should describe the results of each of the three or four segments of your lesson.

3. QUESTIONS. Answer the following questions:
   What did my child learn today?
   What does my child need to learn next?
   What did I learn today?
   What do I need to learn next to teach my child?

Questions or Concerns:

   I designed this Sullivan Report Format to guide my students' organization of their time with the children. I don't want them to write formal lesson plans that require behavioral objectives; they aren't in a position to determine what their children need until they have had the chance to work with them and assess their strengths. Also, within the hour and fifteen minutes that they will be working with their new buddies, they will have to introduce and teach a number of lessons. Constructing an outline under each section of the Sullivan Report allows them to focus not only on teaching an appropriate lesson but also on keeping track of their children's as well as their own learning needs. It will introduce them to the role of the teacher as researcher and reflective practitioner, a role in which they will learn to collect and reflect upon anecdotal information.

When Glenda Bissex (1987) wrote, "A teacher researcher may start out not with a hypothesis to test, but with a wondering to pursue" (3), she could well have been describing my students' interactions with the children each week. Each year, from the moment they are paired with the children, my students bond and feel a deep sense of responsibility to them. When they write to me each week, they are in a constant state of wondering, searching, and trying to understand how they can truly reach and teach these children.

Much of the literature surrounding journal writing suggests that instructors should check or respond to their students' journals only occasionally. Reading and responding to the three sections of my students' folders after each class is intensely time consuming. I have found it such a valuable tool for monitoring my students' progress and for formulating future instruction, however, that I think that immediately responding to each piece of writing is time well spent.

When my students come into each class, they will pick up their manila folders, slip in whatever they need to for the day, write to me at the end of class, and return the folders to me on their way out. Building this routine into our classes will force my students to take responsibility for their own learning. They must reflect and write about what they learn during each class; they must read, react to assignments, and come prepared for class discussion; and they must decide what to teach each week and reflect upon their successes and failures.

This will be our fifth fall working Wednesday mornings with the first-grade children at Sullivan School. Instead of the original four classrooms, however, there are now only two first grades. The navy is gradually moving out of Newport, and this is reducing the number of children who attend Sullivan. Also, a new Early Childhood Center has been created in another section of Newport; some of the children and their teachers have been transferred there.

Over the years, the first-grade teachers and I have discovered that in order for the program to be truly effective, my students must work *one-on-one* with the first graders. This allows them to provide individual attention, tailor instruction, and monitor weekly progress. Since there are thirty-four first graders and this semester I have thirty-six students, we will invite two students from a multiage classroom to complete our sets of buddies.

My Students Arrive

This semester, like years before, a group of energetic young women enter my class charged to learn how to teach children to read. Represented among them are students from Massachusetts, New Jersey,

Connecticut, New Hampshire, New York, Hawaii, Tennessee, Florida, and Rhode Island. They have attended public, private, and Catholic secondary schools and graduated in classes ranging from 27 to 850 students. This combination should provide a variety of learning histories that we can share.

As we sit in a circle during our first week of classes I ask them, "So how did you learn to read?" Many can't remember. It's often that way for those who didn't have any trouble. But then they begin to generate memories:

> All I can remember is reading a book to my mother, "See Spot run."

Others also remember the famous Dick and Jane. One mentions programmed kits,

> All I remember are those books that had the answers on the right side. I had to get my answers cut out because I used to just look at the answers and not even read what the book said.

Other students respond,

> I recall the teachers asking the students to sound out the pronunciation of the letters of the alphabet and having us read words with the same sounds in the endings—for example: *cat, hat* and *book* and *hook.*

> I learned to read through reading groups and through phonics books.

> I was in a group too, the Cardinals.

One student adds,

> I was very shy and hated speaking in front of other people, so when it came to reading I was put in the "slowest" reading group. I felt that this labeled me as stupid and took away from my self-confidence. I was always embarrassed when it came to reading time. Then I was moved up to the next higher reading group and I felt a little better about myself, but I felt like I was abandoning my friends. I think that started off all of my bad experiences with reading.

Some mention their families as primary influences on their beginning reading,

> My parents and older siblings read to me a great deal when I was young. I learned stories by heart. I began to associate certain pictures in the books with certain parts of the story. After a while I could recognize words that kept popping up throughout the story. By the time I got to school, I knew some words and most of the letter sounds.

It seems that most of their learning histories reflect traditional reading instruction. I wonder about their current perceptions of themselves as readers. I ask, "How would you describe yourself as a reader?" One volunteers,

> I'm an avid reader of romance novels and biographies of famous people. I know my choice of books is not very educational.

Another picks up on the theme,

> I'm a good reader. I read quickly probably because I've read so much. What I read is hardly ever educational though. I like to read for enjoyment.

They view school reading and pleasure reading as two separate categories, and I sense they feel guilty when they are not reading the punitive school variety. Another adds without guilt,

> I love to read and also to be read to—even at age twenty-nine. I read about thirteen books over this past summer in the back yard under our mango tree.

Several, however, reveal past and present difficulties with reading,

> I presently hate it! It is almost painful. It makes my eyes hurt, it makes me very tired and I read very slowly. I have poor reading comprehension. With a reading assignment of one chapter it can take me up to twelve hours, not all at once. I often feel I work a lot harder than others and end up getting less out of the reading than others who find it less difficult to read.

Another student adds,

> I can read well out loud but two minutes after, I have a difficult time remembering what I read.

There's quite a contrast among members of the class. I've got to get some students more enthused about reading this semester, and maybe through this course I'll be able to teach some strategies that will help some improve their own comprehension.

I ask them about what they've been reading lately. One comments,

> I'm not an avid reader. I wish I read a lot more because after I finish a book I feel so good.

Another adds,

> I know what you mean. Lately I've found myself taking an interest in autobiographies, so I've been buying those books. I even have a preferred customer card at Waldenbooks.

Some admit that they read only when it is required. Another comments,

> Until recently, I had never enjoyed reading and actually did everything in my power to avoid it. About a year ago while I was in a bookstore, I picked up a novel that I had heard people talking about and bought it. From the day I began that book, I realized how informative, relaxing, and enjoyable reading can be. Now I read whenever I have the time.

They begin to share book titles they've read within the past year: *The Joy Luck Club, The Pelican Brief, Growing up Female, The Client, Crime and Punishment, The Bridges of Madison County, A Woman Named Jackie, SeinLanguage, Schindler's List, The Read Aloud Handbook.* They chat about their favorite authors: John Grisham; Robert Fulhgrum; Stephen King; Sidney Sheldon; and Danielle Steele. They also discuss some children's books they've read for other classes or that they've read to nieces and nephews.

Our discussion eventually leads to teaching, "At this point, how would you teach a child to read?" I ask.

> I would teach a child to read the same way I learned—by sounding out the letters in the alphabet and sounding out words that lend themselves to beginning readers.

> I would teach them the phonics of each individual letter and how to put them together forming a word. Then I would show them how to place and read those words in a sentence structure.

> I think that vocabulary flash cards that familiarize students with not only how the word looks but also what it means are helpful.

The majority of my students emphasize drill with letters and the use of phonics. This reflects how they were taught. Several, however, offer different suggestions and a spark of hope.

> I would begin read-alouds at an early age. Let the child follow along with you in the book. The child should be persuaded eventually to read along or create his or her own story to go along with the pictures, even if the words are not exactly right.

> You must first teach a child to love reading. A child will not want to learn if she does not see a purpose to it. Reading should be fun right from the start. A teacher should model the same type of excitement that she would like to see in her students' eyes.

From our discussion, I can see that most of my students learned to read in a traditional manner with basal readers, groups, workbooks, and programmed reading kits. They learned from teachers who placed emphasis on skills and, in some cases, from teachers who turned them off to reading. I've got to get them to convince themselves by the end of the semester that there is more than phonics to help children learn to read, and that they can learn to teach reading with methods different from those their teachers used with them.

Before I send my students to Sullivan next week, I also need to know their perceptions of what it means to be a student at risk. I ask them to write their definition of what *at-risk* means. Among their responses they offer:

> At-risk means any student who has problems in school and at home that affect their performance in the classroom. These students might have a hard time adjusting to and trusting others.

> These are children who have hard lives. The situations in their lives are not conducive to learning. Often an at-risk child is plagued with the worries of an adult and education loses its importance; daily survival and emotional strain make these children at risk of losing the game of life before they even have a chance to play.

I feel comfortable with their initial awareness of and sensitivity to at-risk children. Now I need to determine what teaching experience, if any, my students have had. Of the thirty-six, only two describe themselves as having no previous teaching experience. The rest have taught children through a variety of situations. Some baby-sat, worked as nannies, or assisted at day care centers. Others taught Catechism, worked as camp counselors, or assisted elementary school teachers through special programs. Three tutored sixty hours each through a course we offer at the university. One had worked as a substitute in Massachusetts, and another had been hired as a general math teacher in a summer school in Hawaii.

I find this information helpful because the first-grade teachers and I no longer randomly place the children with my students. Instead, we reserve two weeks at the beginning of the semester to each get to know our own students. If I notice I have a student who seems to lack confidence, we try to match him or her with an outgoing first grader (or vice versa). We pair elementary ESL students with university students who have studied their language or who want to learn more about working with children from other countries. We also give university students who have double majors in special and elementary education the opportunity to work with children who exhibit a need for extra help either academically or emotionally. We also match some of the more difficult children with my students who have had more teaching experience.

During the first two weeks of the semester, I also familiarize my students with an overview of appropriate books to read to first graders. I stress the use of picture books, *I Can Read* books, and books with rhythm and repetition. I also introduce them to nonfiction books which appeal to some children. Besides encouraging my students to visit our curriculum library, I urge them to take advantage of the wonderful books available at the Newport Public Library.

Since small-grant money is no longer available from my university, I ask my students to buy white paper, construction paper, markers, crayons, a paper punch, a stapler, scissors, plastic alphabet letters, index cards, margarine tubs, glue, or any other materials they think they will need to construct books and extension activities. They also must bring a shoe box for each of the children. They will help the children to decorate it and use it as a storage area for all the books, journals, drawings, and games they create together. These boxes remain in the classroom, and the children can review their contents throughout the week if they choose. Bringing our own materials and children's literature books each week reduces the burden on the Sullivan School budget, increases the children's exposure to a variety of reading materials, and keeps the children focused and motivated to learn. It also allows my students to create lessons on the spot if what they have planned fails.

Within the first two weeks our communication system is functioning, they've collected their children's literature books, they've prepared their first lessons with materials, and I've assigned them the names of their new buddies. The next time I see them will be at Sullivan School, where they will meet their buddies and the challenges of the semester.

Chapter Six

Four Stories

When I place a Salve student with a Sullivan child, I draw together two very special individuals with different backgrounds, sets of abilities, and interests. What each child and Salve student learns as a result of this pairing is unique to the combination. If I matched them in different ways, very different learning outcomes might result. Let's eavesdrop on some of this semester's buddies.

Jenna and Mic

Jenna is tall and slim with long, silky blonde hair parted in the middle. As she sits in class she reminds me of one of the young girls you would see on the beach in California. At the beginning of the semester, when my students share how they learned to read, Jenna stands out as a student who grew up with a traditional basal system and "endured" reading. She reflects:

> As I was growing up, my teachers used the basal, very structured. The classroom was quiet, no interaction. We only did worksheets and workbooks. I always felt guilty if I asked someone what they got for an answer. Then you'd get in trouble and get sent to the back of the room. The way I was taught made me negative about reading. I was always being graded on my opinion and if it didn't match the teacher, you got it wrong. You didn't have a say in anything. You couldn't express yourself. It was like you were pretending to be someone that your weren't just to get a good grade.

I begin to watch her more closely. During the next several weeks as my students first read about whole language, we discuss the difference between a student-centered and a teacher-centered environment.

This is a foreign concept for Jenna, but one that makes an impact upon her thinking. In one reading reaction she writes:

> When I was in school we did things by ourselves with mastery learning. I received direct instruction where the teacher provided us with background information on a topic and asked the questions. I would rather have been taught indirectly where the teacher is the facilitator rather than the provider of knowledge.

Throughout every class Jenna remains focused and asks good questions. From her comments I can tell that this course is making her aware of a completely new way to approach the teaching of reading. She notes:

> I also believe that poor reading can be blamed on poor text and poor teaching. Some teachers cannot teach reading positively and when that happens the child finds it so difficult to read and winds up not even wanting to read. The teacher cannot force a child to read a certain way. They have to be flexible and allow the child to learn however they are comfortable. How can you teach reading to children so they will think positively and not negatively about it?

I see that Jenna is concerned that she might treat her new buddy like she was treated in elementary school and thus turn him off to reading. Like so many of my students, she tells me that she is nervous. She's had experience with children but hasn't taught reading. As the first meeting with her buddy approaches, she writes in her class reaction:

> I learned today that I need to be a very organized and responsible person. I am going to be very important to my buddy and I cannot let him down. When I go to Sullivan School and work with my buddy, I am going to allow time for him to express his feelings and talk to me about what he is learning and what he wants to learn.

She's ready. On our first visit with our buddies, Jenna is paired with Mic, a sweet little boy with short-cropped brown hair and big brown eyes. I see them talking and he sits reservedly, glancing down at his desk from time to time. Occasionally he peeks at Jenna from the corner of his eye and grins. I wait for her first summary Sullivan Report to get her impressions:

> My first day at Sullivan went great. I met my buddy and we talked about his family and how he likes to play t-ball. We decorated his box so he can put all his work into it. I read a book to him and he echoed some words. He wrote the alphabet but he made some letters backwards. He recognized the letters and kind of knows the sounds they make but we will have to work on sounds of consonants

and vowels. We need to work on putting simple words together and
sounding out the letters of the alphabet. It will be challenging but
successful.

We tend to teach as we were taught. Jenna's teachers used a bottom-
up approach that stressed phonics, infallible decoding, and the need to
put simple words together to form sentences. Whether intentionally
or not, Jenna resorts to this same approach with her buddy.

Another hurdle that is difficult for Jenna and so many of my students to overcome is the fact that a teacher doesn't have to correct
every mistake a child makes. My students worry that they aren't
fulfilling their obligation as teachers if they let children make mistakes.
They fear that children's mistakes will become branded in their memory forever. However, as we continue our class discussions, Jenna
moves further away from her traditional background. She writes:

> Miscues don't mean you are a bad reader; they mean you are nor-
> mal. A teacher can't always correct the miscues a child makes
> because this will discourage the child from continuing to read. If the
> miscue has no affect on the meaning, let it go.

But in spite of these observations, Jenna soon decides that she wants
Mic to work on letter recognition and sounds, and to begin to put
words together. She writes,

> I have flashcards with letters on them so we can make words and
> sound them out.

In my response, I caution her about focusing on words in isolation
and stressing the alphabet too much. She needs to work more with
whole text. When she submits her second Sullivan Report she has
accommodated my suggestions:

> We read the book *Old Black Fly* by Jim Alesworth. This was an ABC
> book that we read last week. Mic echo read some words after me. He
> was able to identify all the letters of the alphabet—even the letters
> he had trouble with last week. We then read *Monster Tracks* by A.
> Delaney. He enjoyed this book because there were many pictures
> that he could elaborate on. He made up stories about each picture.
> When we finished the book we discussed it and he understood it. I
> made flashcards of letters and he put his name together.
>
> He doesn't know any sight words because I put simple words
> together and he didn't even know the word "I". Then we made an
> "I like" book. I wrote *I like* and he copied it. He wrote in his journal
> and drew a picture.
>
> Today I learned that I cannot be a bottom up teacher with him.
> He needs to be read to a lot so he is familiar with the whole text. I
> need to learn how to go about teaching him sight words other than
> reading to him. Any suggestions?

Before I get the chance to speak to Jenna she gleans the needed information from her reading of our classroom text. She writes in her next reading reaction:

> In reading the chapter I realized that you can increase your sight vocabulary by being read to. Because I was taught a different way I thought comprehension could take place by memorizing vocabulary. I see how sight vocabulary can be implemented through games, writing, books etc. This chapter gave me great ideas that I can use with my buddy . . .

I wonder how she will respond to the chapter that focuses on phonics. Her comments inform me about her progress and her new-found information:

> I realize that reading isn't just phonics like I learned in elementary school. It has more to do with comprehending what you have read and putting it into meaning that helps you.
>
> I admire the teacher in the chapter who is teaching phonics through whole language. Phonics plays an important role in reading but it could also cause problems if it is taken to the extreme. . . . Children must learn to enjoy reading rather than always concentrating on the phonics.

I look forward to our next week at Sullivan to see if she incorporates what she has learned. Unfortunately, Mic is absent and Jenna works with a new child from the multiage class. Jenna is forced to improvise. They read *Cinderella* and several Sunshine books with predictable language. Her little buddy makes good predictions although she knows no sight words. Using a magnetic board with letters, the little girl spells out her name. I am glad to see that Jenna doesn't focus upon letters and phonics. Instead, she reads to and with the child and lets the child show her what she knows. Jenna makes a quick assessment and knows where to begin.

The next week Mic returns. The first thing he tells Jenna is that he wants to read a book if Jenna will read it to him first. Jenna then uses the Dolch sight-word list to see which words he knows. He doesn't know very many, so they work for the first time with the *at* family. Mic does a good job of placing initial consonants before the phonogram. At the end of the lesson they read *Don't you Laugh at Me!* by Joy Cowley. Jenna comments in her Sullivan Report:

> Mic was able to read the book by himself. Can you believe that? He wanted to read it and he did. I am so proud of him. He added a couple of words in but it didn't change the meaning so I didn't say anything.

In class I discuss the process of scaffolding, a technique that I think Jenna's teachers never employed. Jenna writes:

> I like the idea of scaffolding. The teacher is skillful and acts as an expert. Then she weaves herself away so the children can become more independent learners. It is extremely important for children to be independent and responsible. Now when I am working with my buddy each week he is becoming more independent. He tells me what *he* wants to do and what I should do.

Each week Mic's confidence grows. He initiates activities that Jenna has already modeled for him. One week when Jenna arrives, Mic is busy practicing the words from his word bank. The first thing he says is, "Jen, I know all these cards." I don't think Jenna believes him, but he quickly recites all of them—even the words he learned the first week. Mic then chooses to read a new book called *Ice Cream* by Joy Cowley. Mic continues to surprise Jenna. This week in her Sullivan Report she writes:

> We read a new book—*Ice Cream* by Joy Cowley. He was able to read most of the book alone. I am amazed that two weeks ago he couldn't read one word.

As the semester progresses, Jenna continues to introduce new word families and games to reinforce Mic's sight vocabulary. She not only learns how to teach but also learns more about herself and the reading process. After completing a chapter on comprehension, Jenna writes in her reading reaction:

> I really wasn't taught comprehension strategies. Reading was never a social event; we never got to share and problem solve together. It's important for the classroom teacher to have a classroom discussion. This allows the children to come together and share information. They will learn from each other and get new ideas.

The following week Mic leads the way again. When Jenna arrives, he is reviewing his cards. He knows them all—even the ones he just learned last week. They start to use a magnetic board, and Jenna places words that Mic knows on the board. He reads them with no problem. Then Jenna models creating a sentence with the words on the board. Mic writes the sentences on long strips of oaktag and reads them back with ease. Then he asks if he can create sentences on the board. Working with the *at* family, he creates "Jenna is a bat" and "Mic is a rat." As I walk by I see Mic giggling coyly as Jenna bursts out laughing. "Look what Mic wrote," she says. The magnetic board reads "Jenna is fat." Mic is pleased with his sense of humor, and another pair of Salve/Sullivan buddies joins in the laughter. The little girl adds, "Never tell a teenager she's fat."

Mic and Jenna now work in a predictable routine each week. Mic knows over fifty sight words and he knows he is doing well. He tells Jenna what he does and doesn't want to do, and he works very hard the whole time they are together. Mic is on his way to becoming a successful reader. Jenna is learning to appreciate a new philosophy and approach to teaching reading.

Colleen and José

Colleen's complexion is smooth and fair. In direct contrast, her dark curly hair radiates uncontrollably from the top of her head to rest gently on her shoulders. She's quite outgoing, and when she smiles her eyes twinkle and an impish grin spreads across her face. She tells me that her elementary school had a wonderful literacy program and that she did a great deal of writing and reading all through the years. She says, "I enjoy all types of reading. I read as much as I can and anything I can find." Still, she is nervous. In her first journal entry she writes:

> I feel like we're being thrown into a school and given the command "teach." It is strange that three months ago I was strictly a student; now I feel like I've suddenly (without my knowledge!) been turned into a teacher.

I increase her anxiety when I assign her an ESL student whose native language is Spanish. I think she can handle the situation because I know she has taught kindergarten classes, health to fourth and fifth graders, and even worked with junior high students as part of the SADD program. But when she hears that she'll be working with José, she says, "I'm terrified. I've taken five years of French . . . I'm totally unprepared for this little kid."

As I get to know her, I don't think her initial anxiety will last. Within a few days, she reads her textbook and we begin our class discussions. Her outlook begins to improve:

> The author has put me a bit more at ease. I'm nervous because I understand the importance and lasting effects of what I do with this child. This is going to be a great deal of work and the best part is I'm going to see the direct results. This is no longer "busy work;" this has a purpose.

The first two weeks of the semester I introduce them to the whole language philosophy, the types of books to read to children, how to construct language experience stories, and how to use games like concentration to reinforce letter recognition or sight words. It is like a crash course in a foreign language before visiting the country for the first time. It is impossible to know what their children's needs will be, so I can't be specific about what will work. The ambiguity makes some of my students uneasy. They have to prepare a variety of experiences and use their best judgement when they arrive.

Colleen prepares an activity-packed lesson for her first visit. She plans to create name tags for herself and her buddy and to decorate his shoe box, which will hold their semester creations. Then she wants him to choose a book from among those she'll bring, and she'll read it to him. They'll talk about the book, and she wants him to write about what parts or characters he likes best. After that she'll have him write his name and any other words he knows. They'll review the alphabet and the sounds each letter makes. They will begin to construct the first page of an alphabet book and then return to the book they read aloud to pick out all the letter *A*s. He will practice writing *A* in his journal and then write a review of the day. It's an overwhelming and impossible list to accomplish in an hour and fifteen minutes, but I'm glad to see that she is over- rather than underprepared.

When Colleen gets to Sullivan she meets José. He is really an irresistible little boy, with silky brown bangs that touch the top of his eyebrows. Huge brown eyes complement a quick smile of tiny baby teeth. Within minutes of her arrival, however, reality strikes. Her lesson didn't match his skills. After her first visit she writes in her Sullivan Report:

> When I arrived and met José, I realized that I had prepared for a more advanced child. He can recognize his name and can copy letters very well, but he has no idea what he is copying. He's very funny and friendly and enjoyed drawing. He seems to like animals so I plan to bring a very basic book about animals next week. I was surprised to learn that at the beginning of last year he spoke no English! He speaks very well now. He is obviously a good learner. Although I realize this will be a challenge, I have confidence in José's ability to read.

I'm happy to see that she holds high expectations for her buddy. However, she's also feeling discouraged. In a later discussion she further elaborates on the first visit:

> I talked to him and saw what he knew and what he didn't know. And he didn't know anything. I tried reading him a book and he didn't want to read. He went through my bag and pulled out paper and drew. I said to myself, "I've got to structure this kid. He's all over the place." I left exhausted and very discouraged thinking I don't know what I'm going to do with this kid. He's out of control.

Soon Colleen regroups and decides to start with basic skills by focusing part of her next lesson on the letter *a*. They begin by reading

Where the Wild Things Are and an alphabet book. She works with flash cards and asks José to find *as* in *Where the Wild Things Are*. They next write *as* and trace *as*, and at the end of the lesson she asks him to write an *a* in his journal. He writes a *w*.

In her Sullivan Report, Colleen comes to some conclusions about the direction she should head in:

> He doesn't seem interested in story books. I think the language bar-
> rier is a factor in all of this. He is a very intelligent and enthusiastic
> child. However, I believe he can't grasp the idea that our language
> can be a form of entertainment. We sang the "alphabet song" sev-
> eral times. He likes communicating by singing and drawing. José
> would draw a picture of a bear and I'd say, "What do you hear at the
> beginning?" and he'd say, "ba-ba b." It was an effective game. He
> prints well even though he has no idea what he is actually doing. He
> asked about my name, how to spell it, what it looks like, etc. So he
> wrote "Colleen" and "José" several times.

At the end of the report she formulates plans for her next lesson:

> José needs to hear more of the language. I need to find fast, funny
> books for him. He needs to see words as "labels" rather than ran-
> dom, meaningless pictures. I learned that children have their own
> methods of communication. I honestly believe that José sees no dif-
> ference between my words and his drawings. How do I explain let-
> ters to a child that has heard a completely different language his
> entire life? I've already run into the obvious *j* problem. I need help
> in developing a game he can play to learn his sounds.

She is right, José needs to hear more language. His strongest means of communication is through pictures, which transcend the language barrier. I remind my students not to concentrate on what the children can't do but rather to focus on what they can do. Colleen needs to work through his strengths.

She begins her third lesson by asking José what he would like to do. He says he'd like to draw, so she suggests that they read a book and then he can draw a picture about it. He agrees. He chooses the book, but after a page and a half he wants nothing to do with the book. He says he wants to draw again.

Colleen remembers that last weekend was his birthday, so she asks him to draw a picture of what he did. She labels the pictures. She then attempts to read another book, but he completely ignores her. I can see she is becoming discouraged. She introduces an alphabet game that involves matching letters with pictures of items that begin with those letters. Again, José loses interest after about ten letters. Colleen notes one flicker of hope, however, at the end of her Sullivan Report:

He spoke about dinosaurs a lot. Next week I plan to use three very simple, nicely illustrated dinosaur books. I'm making a dinosaur poster with dinosaur eggs with letters of the alphabet on them so he can practice. Since he always wants to draw and sometimes ignores me when I ask him to talk about what he is drawing, I am bringing my Shel Silverstein poetry books to read. He will at least hear the language while he is drawing.

During week four, the breakthrough occurs. Colleen's giant green dinosaur poster attracts José's attention. He places all the letter eggs on the parts of the dinosaur with the corresponding letters. He runs around the classroom to show his accomplishments to his friends. Next Colleen reads him *Dinosaur Day* and *Dinosaur Garden*. When she finishes reading, José notices that the books are written by the same author and illustrator. He points to the word *dinosaur* in both titles and says, "These are the same, see?" He then opens both books and looks through them at the same time to find the differences.

After this, Colleen and José read *It's Halloween* three times. José is talking, asking questions, and predicting what is going to happen on the next page. He remembers illustrations from previous pages and points out the characters and names them. Then Colleen opens to the middle of her poetry book and starts to read. José interrupts her and says, "No, you did it wrong. You start here." He takes the book from her, turns to the first page, and gives it back. After Colleen's fourth visit with José, I notice a more positive outlook in her Sullivan Report reflections:

> He seems to work much better if I have a theme for the day. I learned that teaching isn't easy and that kids are full of surprises. Last week he didn't know *a* and wouldn't let me read more than two pages from a book. Something "clicked" today, and I'm practically in tears, I'm so happy for both of us. I need to learn to develop themes and I need to maintain a friendly, safe, and trusting relationship with José. He is such a fighter and I want to make sure he gets anything and everything he wants or needs from me.

She is learning the powerful role a child's interests must play if she is to build effective lessons. She also realizes the need to make lessons meaningful by concentrating on concepts like dinosaurs rather than on isolated skills like learning the letter *A*.

Each week as I read my students' Sullivan Reports, I search for important breakthroughs like Colleen's. I also jot down notes about creative lessons that made impacts on children, and record questions or concerns my students have that might affect everyone. During class I raise these issues and have my students discuss their successes, failures, and suggestions for improvement. I try to weave theory into their practical experiences so they don't learn in a vacuum. Those who have children with similar needs borrow ideas from each other. They learn to rely on each other.

As Halloween approaches, Colleen develops a Halloween theme. She creates a Halloween poster and brings back *It's Halloween* as part of her lesson. José is able to recognize most of the pictures from the book. He doesn't remember the word *goblin*, but he remembers reading about one last week in another book. He refers to that book and finds the correct page. He copies all of the Halloween words and is able to match these flashcards with the words on Colleen's poster. Then he decides that he wants to make his own book. A first.

José sees other buddies at his table constructing books in the shape of pumpkins, and he wants to do the same. He writes the word *pumpkin* at the top of each page and then dictates a sentence to Colleen. He runs to show me his book and to read the pages as best he can. From her work with José this week, Colleen makes the following observations:

> I'm going to stick with using a theme for my lessons. José has a very short attention span, and themes keep his interest. I need help developing a method to work on José's letter recognition. He knows that words are names, but he doesn't know letters and their relationship to words. I need help. I can't find a way to make this interesting enough to hold his short, little attention span!

The next week Colleen is prepared to continue with her Halloween theme. No luck. José is absent. Colleen works with a girl named Ellie from the multiage class and experiences a new phenomenon. She writes to me in her Sullivan Report:

> José was absent! I was very disappointed. I carried out my lesson plan but I ran into some problems because Ellie was so much more advanced than José. I didn't have enough for her. Lucky for me I was sitting next to Lisa, who always has fantastic ideas and lessons. She slipped me another Halloween book before I lost Ellie. Ellie knew the book and was reading along with the parts she remembered. It was such a different experience. I thought, "Oh my God, this kid wrote two books and read three books." I thought, "What am I going to do?" I learned that children are so different and that a good teacher should be prepared for everything. I was glad that I had ideas from class and my classmates in my head. Flexibility and adaptability are thankfully gifts of mine. I still did feel unprepared and therefore a bit guilty. I can't blame myself, but I learned a lesson. I guess that's what education is all about!

By her next visit, José returns. He immediately takes *It's Halloween*, sits in Colleen's lap, turns the pages, and begins to read to her. He isn't reading the words, but he uses what he can remember from the book along with the picture clues. Colleen helps him with the words *haunted house*, which trigger a memory. José jumps up, grabs another book about a haunted house from his classroom library, and begins to read that book to Colleen. When she writes to me this week, Colleen adds:

> José has come a long way. When he read to me I was almost crying. He'd never done this before. He'd never shown an interest in reading. I remember the first day I was there I brought all the books I liked when I was little like *Corduroy* and *Miss Nelson* and he pushed them all aside and said, "I'm sick of you and your books." Now he is learning why we read and what reading can do for us! You can see yourself breaking through.

It is always rewarding when a breakthrough occurs. I can see a sense of pride on both their faces.

Mattie and Serena

Mattie is unique to my class for several reasons. First, she is an older student, married, and has a four-year old child. She was educated in Tennessee and just recently moved to Rhode Island. She already has a bachelor's degree and is returning to the university to earn a second degree in elementary education. Her background as an African American female and as a mature adult influences the way she interprets experiences.

I could listen to Mattie talk all day. Her soft southern accent and graceful manner endear her to her classmates. She wears her black hair pulled back in a small ponytail. She's quick to laugh and often expresses her emotions by raising her eyebrows and opening her eyes wider and wider.

Mattie's first impression of Sullivan School differs from most of my students'. She makes some observations during a conversation we have at my office:

> You hear so much about the at-risk Sullivan School I expected it to be one way. I expected Sullivan to fit more into a stereotype. When I hear at-risk, I think of metal detectors, a high rate of illiteracy, a lot of children that don't show up for school, and a lot of parents who won't participate. There's no available structure to help students that are in trouble.
>
> It was different. In contrast, Sullivan has Head Start right in the school, they have outreach right in the school, and they have college students who come in and work with the students one-on-one. Going by the schools I've been in and places I've seen in South Carolina and Tennessee, Sullivan is probably a lot closer to what a lot of schools in the U.S. are like. The Sullivan kids are probably

experiencing a lot of the problems a lot of kids face today. Because these kids at Sullivan have all these services it didn't seem so at-risk.

Mattie talks about the impressions and prejudices people can construct from their expectations:

> Sometimes people have a danger of seeing children who have certain needs almost like they are a different animal, almost as if they are not like other children. Maybe I take it a little too personally. I know what it's like to be in an environment where people come in with what they think you're like. They have these ideas of what your problems are, what your home lives are like, what you probably need—without even knowing you. Sometimes people see that and they don't even see you. It's like you are invisible—you can be in an environment where you're not really there. You are there but you're not really a part of it because they focus on what they think you need or want more so than what your needs might be.

It is easy to go to Sullivan with preconceived notions about what the children are like and what they will need. We all do it. Maybe we focus too much on the at-risk factor. I will be sure to ask my students about their thoughts regarding this issue after they've had some time to interact with their children.

Like the rest of her classmates, Mattie comes prepared for her first visit with her buddy, Serena. The little girl greets Mattie with the reserved manner of a very thoughtful and introspective child. She appears older than her years. As they begin by making their name tags, Serena writes her name using capital and lowercase letters. She tells Mattie about her summer vacation, her parents, sisters, and brothers. She says she likes to read and that her parents read to her all the time.

In her sack, Mattie carries every skillbook from her four-year-old son's collection. She shares books about numbers, the alphabet, colors, and shapes as she tries to get an idea of Serena's knowledge. Serena confidently moves through *all* the books, puts them in order, and explains the content. Mattie asks her if she can write any numbers, and Serena turns her name tag over and writes the numerals from one to thirty-five. Some of the numbers are backwards but all are in order.

Mattie begins to read *Quentin Needs Quiet* and Serena fills in the missing words. Then Serena reads *Green Eggs and Ham* to Mattie. She knows most of the story by heart. Initially, she misses a few sentences because she is reciting the book mostly from memory. Mattie takes an index card and places it under the sentences. Immediately, Serena begins to concentrate more on the actual words. She only has trouble with the words *should* and *would*.

Mattie pulls out *The Very Quiet Cricket*. Serena likes the pictures but is even more intrigued with the microchip that makes a chirping sound. She asks, "How did that little thing get in the book? How does it make that noise? Where is it?"

When the first session is over, Mattie reflects on her experience:

> I had every book on every skill and strategy you could think of: colors, shapes, sounds, fill-in-the-blank, and rhyming words. She went right through them. When she picked up *Green Eggs and Ham* I thought, "That's a lot of pages to read when this child might not know all the sounds." She was just going! I was overwhelmed. I said to myself, "See, now you are being guilty of this perception that this kid is going to need all these things. OK, now what are you going to do with her next week?" I didn't have to worry for long. Before I left she told me what she wanted to do the next week. I thought, "That's fine with me." She's something.

On Mattie's next visit, Serena begins by decorating her shoe box. She selects pink, red, and black construction paper and picks up the stapler. Within seconds she switches to a glue stick. Mattie lets her buddy take the lead. Serena molds each piece of paper to the box by folding it and then cutting along the fold. When she finishes cutting and pasting, she writes *My Box*. She writes her own name on one side and asks Mattie to write hers on the other.

Next they make journals. Mattie explains to Serena that she can write whatever she likes in her journal at the end of each class. Mattie and Serena decide that each week they will give her parents a card on which they will list all their weekly accomplishments. Serena picks an index card for this purpose and writes her name at the top.

Then Serena reads *Green Eggs and Ham.* Toward the end of the book, Mattie joins in and they choral read. Mattie reads *Poems for Small Friends,* and Serena is able to use the picture clues to predict what each poem will be about. Serena tells Mattie that she likes listening to poetry. Mattie reads another book and then together they choral read, take turns, and echo read parts of *The Cat in the Hat.* At the end of the lesson Serena writes her first journal entry, "I like my box."

Mattie's Sullivan Report summarizes their experiences. She also adds:

> I would like to know how to stretch what Serena already knows but I still haven't been able to assess how much she knows. So far each activity has been completed with (seemingly) ease. I was surprised by her decision to express herself by writing in her journal. I didn't say she had to write. I told her to do whatever she wanted to remember what she enjoyed most about today's activities. Writing was her choice.

Sometimes an advanced child is more difficult for my students to assess. Weekly experiences dash preconceived ideas about the abilities of first graders. Finding the right instructional level might take several visits.

During their next session, Serena writes her first book. She draws the cover and titles the book *I Like Pumpkins*. She writes three sentences in the book and asks for help in spelling *monster* and *moving*. After that she wants to read *The Little Red Hen*. The reading is a bit difficult so Mattie reads the story to her. While they are reading, Loryn and her little buddy from the other first-grade class come in to meet Mattie and Serena. Through discussion on campus we discovered that these two little girls are both quite advanced. Mattie thought that maybe they could become pen pals and write to each other every week. Serena says she wants to finish reading before she will talk with the other first grader. She sets her mind to business and doesn't want to be interrupted until she has completed a task. Eventually, the children agree that they would like to correspond with each other and Loryn and her buddy leave. Serena and Mattie continue with their lesson.

As the weeks progress, Mattie observes Serena and begins to sharpen her ability to respond to the child's needs. Mattie scours her text to find answers and suggestions—both usually lead to more questions. Mattie is a very independent student, much like the child she is tutoring. At times she proposes two completely different lessons and asks for my opinion as to which would be more effective. She is sometimes torn between what she thinks Serena needs and what she thinks might challenge her. As I deal with Mattie, who works with an advanced child, and other students whose children have unique needs, I find that quick personal conferences at the end of class or individual responses to their class reactions is the most efficient and effective way to meet needs on a weekly basis.

Mattie designates a portion of her next lesson to building Serena's sight vocabulary. She notices several words that Serena missed when reading, so she's prepared a word bingo game. When she arrives, she finds that Serena is late. She works instead with another child, Jane, whose Salve buddy is absent. Like Jenna and Colleen discovered, working unexpectedly with a new student provides Mattie with new challenges and a chance to think on her feet. Mattie glides naturally into a lesson. She applies what we discussed about prereading strategies and leads the child to make predictions. Through quick observation she determines that the child cannot read, so she decides to echo read. They discuss the story as they go, and she guides the child to use the picture clues.

Halfway through the lesson Serena arrives, so Mattie brings out the bingo game. The children help each other with the words they don't know and then read to each other books they have written in previous weeks. Next they make books of their own. Power Rangers is the topic. Mattie writes in her report:

> Instead of getting bored, Serena wanted to do everything Jane did. Jane couldn't write sentences but she dictated sentences to me to correspond with the pictures she drew. Serena wrote in her book what she heard Jane dictate to me. Serena seemed motivated by Jane. Students *do* learn more from each other.

I find that Mattie has no trouble adapting to any situation. She is a natural-born teacher. Her intuitive abilities and inquisitive nature combine to draw children into exciting experiences. Mattie is always excited about what she learns each week and how she sees theory translate into practice before her eyes.

As part of their next lesson, Mattie and Serena make a book of numbers. They place items like macaroni on each page and Mattie writes the name of the item while Serena writes the numeral and word for the number beside each. She spells them *one, tow, tree, for*. This situation raises concerns for Mattie. She writes to me:

> Two things I noticed about today's activities—
> 1) Serena knows words *much* better in a story or sentence than when a word is presented alone (concentration game)
> 2) Serena recognizes words when she sees them in print but spells them differently when she relies on how words sound to her (*tow* for *two* and *for* for *four*). For next week I hope to find a book about numbers where the numbers are spelled out. . . .

When Mattie returns the following week, she reads *Count with Me 1,2,3* to Serena. When they finish, Serena begins to compare the spelling of the numbers in the book to the way she spelled them in her own book. While Mattie comes to get me to explain what's happening, Serena methodically reviews each number. Where she has made a spelling error in her own book, she erases and corrects her mistake. Mattie is impressed with Serena's ability to recognize her mistake and her strategies for finding out how to rectify the situation. Mattie decides that homonyms should be part of her next lesson. She is becoming a facilitator of instruction.

The next week Mattie reviews the words for the numbers and rereads *Count with Me 1,2,3*. They play concentration with the words for numbers one through five, then add six through ten. Mattie then leads Serena to see the difference between the words *two* and *to*. They talk about the use of both. Mattie introduces two books that she has created: one focuses on the word *to* and the other focuses on the word *two*. By tracing the words, filling in the blanks, and then making up sentences using the correct form of *two* and *to,* Serena learns the difference between the homonyms.

As Mattie works with Serena, she continues to be amazed each week by what this child can accomplish. Serena does not typify an at-risk student. It is a fortuitous match because Mattie and Serena constantly challenge each other's zone of proximal development.

AnnMarie and Carl

AnnMarie pulls back her long brown hair and secures it with a barrette. She flashes a genuine smile. In addition to studying elementary education, she is minoring in art. She also works part-time at a local hotel, so her days are full of commitments. Often when I arrive to class early, she and Mattie await me. AnnMarie is very conscientious about her responsibilities, but first appears hesitant and cautious in class. Her own past experiences with reading become clear to me as she writes in one of her reading reactions:

> I remember that my teachers in grammar school used to give reading awards to the student who read the most books at the end of each month. I was a very slow reader and couldn't keep up with the other students so I got turned off by reading. When I came to a word I could not pronounce, my teacher would make me sound out the word until I got it correct. My face would turn red and my hand would clutch the book. I wouldn't look at anyone and I would wait for my teacher to get frustrated with me so she would ask me to sit down. I never truly learned and understood how to sound out words because I was afraid to make mistakes.

I have had students like AnnMarie before. They label themselves as poor readers and carry all the baggage that former teachers have laid on them. I think she is worried about helping her child.

AnnMarie doesn't contribute to class discussion very often at the beginning of the semester. When she does, however, she speaks with sincerity and passion about issues that concern her. One of the first chapters we read discusses the importance of the classroom environment to a child's learning. Apparently AnnMarie's former experiences in not-so-happy classrooms cause her to highlight a few items in her reading reaction:

> —Self-esteem is a vital element in the learning of communication skills.
> —Children's attitudes need to be a priority when learning to read.
> **Saying the right things to my buddy, encouraging him, and making him feel confident is extremely important to me!**

At Sullivan, I pair AnnMarie with Carl because his teacher has warned me of his often rambunctious nature. I take advantage of the fact that AnnMarie has worked with inner-city kids from Hartford. I think she can handle the situation.

After she meets Carl, who looks like an angel you might see in a Sunday School's Christmas play, AnnMarie mentions that he is very shy. She can't determine what he likes to do, what books he likes, or if he likes to draw. When she does get him to draw, he spends a lot of time drawing very detailed pictures. She notices he has a speech problem, and she ends her first Sullivan Report with,

> I need to learn what I can do to help him with his speech.

I caution her about paying attention to his speech. Although she has a tough time understanding him, if she focuses on his speech she might cause him to freeze up and not communicate at all. She takes my advice. The next time she writes:

> I am trying to echo read with my student. Carl has a speech problem but I ignore it because he reads better when you don't remind him.

Although it bothered AnnMarie that her own teachers corrected her every error, she doubts the value of invented spelling. She writes:

> Isn't it important to stop children when they misspell words? Shouldn't you let students explore words but then teach them how to spell them correctly?

AnnMarie admits that she isn't that strong a speller. It concerns her that Carl might turn out the same way. Consequently, what she perceives as her duty as a teacher conflicts with her strong desire to ensure that Carl develops a positive attitude toward reading and writing. She's torn.

The next time she returns to Sullivan, AnnMarie and Carl read the story *Animals in Winter*. She has him predict what the story will be about by identifying objects on the cover. He not only predicts that the book will talk about animals in winter, but as they read he talks about most of the animals and whether or not he has seen them in zoos. Next they make a book cover about the book, and Carl draws his favorite animal in the story. Then they create sentences: "I like bears." "I like birds." "I like wolves." Carl returns to the story to find these words in the text. He is proud of the words he knows and can pick them out himself. Finally, he colors his box and places the book cover in it.

On her next visit AnnMarie comes prepared, but Carl isn't interested in anything. He doesn't want to draw, write, or read. He keeps moving his elbow, causing his crayons to crash to the floor. Then he drops a pile of books. AnnMarie remains calm and doesn't get angry. She laughs and says, "Do you want to sit on the floor?" Nothing gets accomplished that day. Later AnnMarie tells me, "He just wasn't into the work. That's when I got scared and thought, 'I'm just not going to get through to him.'"

There are a number of children like Carl each year who wiggle, fidget, and try to avoid reading and writing. Sometimes my students take it personally and think they are poor teachers—especially when others around them boast of their children's successes. It often helps when we hold workshop sessions that allow my students to come together simply to share their problems. When they listen to what others have to endure, they feel better and less alone. Very often those who *have* had successes share what they have read and games they have created that worked. They boost each other's spirits.

The next week AnnMarie brings an alphabet book and *I Know An Old Lady Who Swallowed a Fly*. Carl loves them. He memorizes the phrase *I Know An Old Lady Who Swallowed a Fly* and repeats it as AnnMarie reads. Then Carl chooses five words from the story for AnnMarie to write on index cards. Carl does the same on his index cards. They play memory with the words. Carl has a difficult time because he doesn't have the context as an aid. He becomes distracted by others around him. The rest of the time is lost.

AnnMarie doesn't give up. The following week she returns with a good lesson plan built around *I Know an Old Lady Who Swallowed a Fly*. She has copied the book and intends to have Carl circle all the words he knows. She has created sentence strips to match with the story and place in order. Then they will cut up the sentence strips and reconstruct them. She has several other books ready for read-alouds. Disappointment. Carl doesn't feel well and doesn't want to do anything. He looks tired, his nose is running, and he puts his head down on the desk. It appears that everything AnnMarie tries sparks no interest. Out of desperation, AnnMarie finally takes out some index cards with pictures of Halloween items (witch, candy, broom) and their corresponding words. They play concentration. Carl not only pays attention but becomes engrossed in the process. When they follow up by reading a book about Halloween, Carl is able to pick out the Halloween-related words. It is the first time Carl has shown enthusiasm for AnnMarie's efforts.

In class we've been talking about literature and how children need to make choices, so the next week AnnMarie brings seven books, including several "I Can Read" books. She lets Carl decide what to read. He chooses three: *Mark's Bedtime, A to Z,* and *Five Little Monkeys Sitting on a Tree*. They choral read *Mark's Bedtime* and look for specific words in the text. Then AnnMarie explains how to use picture clues to decode words in the second book. Finally, Carl takes over and reads the entire third book on his own. AnnMarie's Sullivan Report describes her elation:

> Carl loved *Five Little Monkeys Sitting on a Tree*. He could read almost every word! He pointed to each word he was on and when he finished a sentence he would look over at me and smile. He wanted to read the story over again, which made me proud because he feels comfortable reading with me. He is starting to do things by himself without asking me to do them for him. I'm going to keep encouraging him to write whatever he wants. I think in the beginning he was afraid to be wrong. He has been with me long enough that he knows I'm not going to correct him every five minutes. I'm looking forward to next week.

AnnMarie has finally found a book that Carl can read. It becomes a staple in every lesson thereafter. She suggests that they create a bingo game with some of the words from his story. He's excited to make the word cards and chooses which words to copy. He also writes the words without AnnMarie's help. He's becoming more independent. After he chooses a word and writes it, he places it on the table and recites all the previous words he's set down. He smiles and goes to find his teacher to show her all the words he knows. Then he invites me to witness his success. The best part of this entire procedure is that when Carl can't remember a word, he looks it up in the story, reads the sentence, and then decodes the word. I can see he is proud of himself because he has conquered a new strategy. When AnnMarie writes this week she adds:

> Before I left, Carl asked me if I was going to be late next week. I told him I would be early! He explained to me that he was sad when I didn't come through the door. I told him that if I wasn't coming I would have called the principal and Carl would be the first to know. I told him I loved being there with him.

Not only is Carl gaining confidence, but so is AnnMarie. She comes well prepared for the next week, and as soon as she enters, Carl announces that he wants to read as many books as possible. They begin with *The Very Busy Spider*. At first AnnMarie reads to Carl, but by the middle of the book he is reading along with her. He is intrigued with the spider and with how he can feel the spider's web on the page. Next they read *Brown Bear, Brown Bear, What Do You See?*. This time Carl comments, "I'm going to show you how to read now!" and reads the whole book, pointing to each word as he goes along. From AnnMarie's expression you can tell she's just about ready to fall off her chair. Then they read *Five Little Monkeys* again. AnnMarie tells me, "I'm ready to hang this book up but it is his favorite—so it has to be part of every lesson." Carl has trouble with a few words but uses the picture clues to help decode. They finish with *Blue Hat, Green Hat* and *In a Red House*. Carl is having trouble with the word *redbird*, so AnnMarie covers the word *bird* and Carl sees what is left. He easily says, "red." Then she covers *red* and he says, "bird." Soon he covers up parts of other words, looking for small words that he knows. He is absorbing strategies in meaningful contexts. When they finish reading they place all the books before them, and Carl picks his favorite for the day. He writes the author's name and the title, which he underlines while telling AnnMarie what the story is about. She writes his summary. Then she reads what she has written, and Carl reads the words he can. Another duo is on their way.

Toward the end of the semester AnnMarie comes to class looking for volunteers. The hotel she works for wants to do some charity work around Christmas. They asked all the employees to contribute suggestions, and AnnMarie's won. As a result, the hotel is inviting the entire Sullivan School for two hours of games and a visit from Santa Claus. AnnMarie is in charge and needs some Salve buddies to help staff the game booths. She admits it's quite a strain because it takes place during exam week, but in spite of the conflict many of my students write their names on her volunteer list. They are an amazing group.

Jenna, Colleen, Mattie, AnnMarie and their buddies are only four of thirty-six learning histories that are evolving this semester. Within the past few months I have followed each set of my Salve/Sullivan buddies—each has an equally rich story to reveal. With only two more teaching sessions at Sullivan remaining, it's time for my students to share a bit more about their lives with the children and to assess the learning they have accomplished together. Our portfolios will play a major role in this process.

Chapter Seven

Lessons Learned

December, 1994

December is a bittersweet time of the semester. We are desperate for Christmas break, but a piece of us doesn't want to let go of all that we've shared and accomplished together. It is a time when my students must examine what they and their children have learned. To help them in this analysis I have them complete portfolios, final Sullivan Reports for the teachers, and a take-home final exam.

Starting Portfolios

We begin our portfolios in October. I introduce my students to my portfolio and take time to chat with them:

> The first part of my portfolio begins with samples of school work that reflect my literate behavior. I couldn't find anything from grammar school, but I found my high school yearbook and photocopied the page that showed me as editor-in-chief. I located some exams I took during my college days: western civilization, philosophy, logic, biology, English, educational measurements, computer science, French, and Italian. I also included an English term paper to show you a sample of my extended writing.

They are interested in these papers because they can relate to taking the very same courses. They are also amused by the fact that I didn't get all *A*s in college. I continue:

> I've also added a copy of the cover page of a thesis I wrote for a CAGS degree, and a copy of the title page of my Doctoral Dissertation.

This gives us a chance to talk about my education and answer questions about advanced degrees. All of my students must earn at least a master's degree to be permanently certified as teachers. I return to sharing my portfolio:

I keep the original portfolio that I created with my students several years ago because it reveals the history of my development as a teacher of this reading course.

> I keep a dated bibliographical list of all the books I read. This helps me keep track of the types of books I read, and if I want to recommend a book to a friend, I can remember the title and author. I often include a photocopy of the cover of a book if I particularly like it. Here is one of *Schindler's List*.

> In another section I save some poems friends gave me and other poems I like. I've included some ten-minute writes I do to explore topics, and some drafts of my work on a book I am writing.

I take an entire class period to share my portfolio because they need to have time to ask questions about me and to clarify how they will go about constructing their own. Finally, I describe the last part of my portfolio:

> In the last section I set my goals. I've included pamphlets from the Swiss Engadin Cross Country Ski Marathon and the Mt. Washington Road Race, two events I participated in during my sabbatical. I want to do both of these races again to keep fit and to better my time. I've included my first successful 9 x 13 enlargement of a black-and-white photo. I'm exploring photography and want to be able to take and develop my own pictures. I've also included the letter I received from a publisher saying they would publish my book.

This day my students see me as a person, not just a professor. We begin to connect. I explain that I have attached an index card to each item in my portfolio to describe why I selected it. I ask my students to do the same. I give them time to think about this project and collect materials. We brainstorm ideas that they might want to include in their portfolios, and many of them can't wait to go home and rummage through their attics to collect treasures. I expect them to take responsibility for the design and execution of their portfolios. I don't grade their portfolios. Instead, I value those portfolios that reflect thoughtfulness and introspection, that represent my students as people, and that will serve as a source of inspiration for future reading and writing.

Sharing Portfolios

In November they bring their portfolios to class to share. As I circulate among their small groups I hear them laughing. Some portfolios include birth certificates, baby and childhood photos with family members, and kindergarten awards. Report cards, standardized test results, and certificates of accomplishment in dance, good behavior, good effort, and spelling decorate the pages. Work samples, finger paintings, drawings, and math tests add richness to their histories. They value their participation in tennis, soccer, track, paddling, basketball, swimming, bowling, and cross-country skiing. Photos, schedules of events, announcements of championships, and newspaper clippings reveal a part of my students that I rarely hear about. They include books they have written as children for the Young Authors' Conferences, and cards from parents and boyfriends. Poems by Emily Dickenson and stubs from rock concerts by Paul Simon all contribute to the description of today's preservice teachers.

A very important part of my students' lives is their involvement in the process of becoming teachers. They include essays they wrote to apply to the university and letters congratulating them upon their acceptance to one or more of the education programs. Scores from Scholastic Aptitude Tests and National Teacher Exams appear in many portfolios. Some students comment on how poorly they did on these tests, yet praise the efforts and accomplishments they've achieved in spite of them.

My students enthusiastically thumb through each other's portfolios. In fact, there isn't enough time to get a glimpse of all of them. They describe to each other why they included items and how certain photos and work samples bring back memories both good and bad. The chance to reconstruct their learning histories makes them more aware of how they were treated and how they wish to treat their future students.

When they went home to collect their portfolio artifacts, the process netted unexpected benefits. One student who constructed her portfolio with her mom and her little sister commented:

> I had no idea that my mom saved my report cards, art work, certificates, and class pictures. It brought back some fantastic memories that made me laugh. My mom works almost seven days a week and at the same time takes care of a family. It seems like she is always on the run. The portfolio gave us the chance to sit down in peace and quiet and laugh.

For other students, the chance to reassemble and reflect upon their lives helped them to appreciate their self-worth:

> I learned that I am a successful person even when I may not be successful on a test. During my life I have always set high goals for myself and I would not give up until I reached them. I have accomplished a lot in my twenty years of living and no one can take that away from me. I am involved in many activities that have helped me become the person I am today, a strong and determined individual.

By constructing their portfolios, they learned how important their families are to them and how both their home and school environments have shaped the way they view the world today.

When my students share their portfolios with each other, it feels as if they are meeting some of their classmates for the first time. Although they've been in some of the same classes together for the past two years, they never really thought about sharing their families, schooling, or upbringing. One student writes:

> Sharing my portfolio with my classmates was fun but sad too. I had such a great childhood and explaining my portfolio brought back so many memories I wish I could live over again. I guess you don't know how much you have accomplished until you make a portfolio and go through the things you put in it.

This is probably one of the most valuable lessons my students learn. Another adds:

> I realized that I was not always able to read and write. I was not born with a book in one hand and a pencil in the other. I look back on my work and I can't believe that I wrote those papers. I almost seemed as if I was a different person and a different child completed all of those worksheets. . . . It made me realize that I'm not that much older than my Sullivan buddy is and I should try to get in touch with old school feelings in order to help my students better.

Helping the Children Build Portfolios

Toward the end of the semester my students bring their portfolios to Sullivan to share their lives with their buddies and to model the use of portfolios as a means of self-evaluation. The little ones smile with glee as they view photos and work samples from my students' days in elementary school. I overhear several comments from the first graders, "I can't believe you used to write that way." "Look at this picture of you, you were chubby." My students share pictures of their families, and the children get a better idea of the university students who visit each week. Some children are fascinated with sports pictures and pour over every detail. They chat incessantly. The children see report cards and awards my students have won. I hear one of my students explain, "I put these things into my portfolios because I am proud of what I have accomplished."

After looking at my students' portfolios, the children are ready to get started on their own. They open their shoe boxes and review all that they have accomplished this semester. They take out games, flashcards, drawings, and journals. Some boxes include turkeys made from hand tracings and Christmas lists that highlight Power Rangers. Lists of books the children have read and homemade books shaped like pumpkins and dinosaurs work their way into plastic sleeves to be secured in three-ringed notebooks. Puppet characters, alphabet books, and name tags do not escape the mighty portfolio.

Most of the children want to place *all* of their work into their portfolios. We agree that this is OK. The children dictate why they have selected various items, and my students write the children's responses on index cards to attach to various pages in their portfolios. A few children respond, "Because I like it." But many describe a definite purpose for each selection: "Because I want to show it to my family"; "So I can use them to teach my kids"; "So I can play this game with my brother and cousin"; "So I can read them and show my mom I can read"; "Hangman is my favorite game and I beat Lori."

Some place items in their portfolio because "It is good work." One wants to include an item done early in the semester because "It shows how I used to write." Another wants to place her journal in her portfolio because "It is important and I don't want to lose it." One little boy comments, "I'm putting this in because this is the last book I made with Denise and she helped me make the pictures, so I like it."

As the children construct their portfolios, they compare work they did at the beginning of the semester with what they accomplished at the end. They are so excited to count all the books they read and to review all the books they wrote. They are learning to measure their own progress.

As soon as they complete their portfolios, the children want to share them with their classmates and the other Salve buddies. They can't talk fast enough. Each is so proud. In her Sullivan Report for this week, AnnMarie comments about helping Carl with his portfolio:

> Carl and I shared portfolios. I showed him some of the things I have done, sports I've played, awards, family pictures etc. Carl had all kinds of questions for me about school and college. He asked me, "What do you do in college? Is it hard? Why do you have to go to college? Why did you get so many awards?"
> I think that Carl learned a little bit of what I'm all about. Next thing I knew he wanted to do his own portfolio.
> While he was going through his box, he amazed himself at how many books we have read together. . . . Throughout the whole time we put together his portfolio he wanted to make sure everything was perfect! I think he was proud of all the work he had done.

Building the children's portfolios serves more than the children. My students have to review all that the children accomplished. They discuss each item, help the children to select what they valued, and decide why each item should be included. After completing the process, one of my students remarks:

> Before we did our student portfolios I felt that I hadn't taught Katy anything. As I began to look through the things she had in her box, I realized how much we actually did do.

Sometimes my students doubt their effectiveness and teaching abilities throughout the semester, but when they review portfolios with the children their strengths, creativity, and dedication become apparent.

One of my students later summed up her feelings about the value of the entire portfolio process for both the university and elementary children. She wrote:

> Portfolios are a way for you to show and share the things you are proud of. With portfolios we can view the way our reading and writing changes over time. It is a way to let people know who and what you are. To show them what you're proud of and to sort of brag a bit.

All of the students agreed.

The Final Sullivan Report

In addition to helping the children construct portfolios, my students must also prepare a Final Sullivan Report that they can share with the parents and ultimately give to the classroom teacher. To do this, my students must review all of their weekly Sullivan Reports and work samples collected in the children's portfolios. It is a time for them to analyze and synthesize what they have taught and what the children have learned since September. I ask them to focus on the positive and to report all the children's strengths, abilities, and accomplishments that they have documented.

Mattie's report illustrates the format and content of the typical Final Sullivan Report that my students write:

FINAL SULLIVAN REPORT

Name: Serena
Grade: 1st
Date: December 14, 1994
Salve Teacher: Mattie

Narrative
Serena is a very bright first grader. She is cooperative, enthusiastic, and fun to be with. She is polite, focused on goals, and possesses a great sense of humor.

Strengths and Abilities
Serena can:
Write her first and last name.
Copy the month, day, and year.

Identify numbers 1–100.
Identify the 26 letters of the alphabet.
Identify color words: (red, yellow, blue, white, black purple, pink, orange, green, brown, gray).
Write numerals 1–34 from memory.
Write the alphabet.
Use picture clues to understand a sentence or story.
Use context clues to unlock words.
Sound out words using phonetic cues.
Use background knowledge to make predictions.
Participate in choral reading.
Read independently.
Sequence the events in a story.
Write complete sentences.
Use capital and lowercase letters appropriately.
Use a period correctly to end sentences.
Construct stories independently.
Identify authors and titles of books.
Use drawings to interpret a story.
Identify the following sight words:
the, was, as, do, to, out, all, be, can, two, his, at, have, could, and, that, him, go, so, he, she, with, we, see, a, for, up, then, my, I, on, look, big, had, you, they, there, down, it, but, some, of.

Books We Have Read Together:
The Cat In The Hat by Dr. Seuss.
The Berenstains' B Book by the Berenstains.
The Very Hungry Cricket by Eric Carle.
The Alphabet Pals' Surprise by World Book, Inc.
The Lost Key by World Book, Inc.
Quentin Needs Quiet by World Book, Inc.
Poems for Small Friends by Bobbi Katz and Gyo Fujikawa.
Doorbell by Jan Pienkowski.
Green Eggs and Ham by Dr. Seuss.
Oh, Kojo! How Could You? by Verna Aardema.
The Little Red Hen (a First Golden Book series).
My Little Book of Poems by Rebecca Heller.
In a Small, Small Pond by Denise Fleming.
I Know an Old Lady Who Swallowed a Fly by Colin and Jacqui Hawkins.
Quack, Quack, Quack! by Joy Cowley.
Mrs. Wishy-washy.
Ice Cream Is Falling! by Shigeo Wanatabe and Yassuo Ohtomo.
Count with Me 1,2,3 by Deborah Bennett D'Andrea.
Dancing with the Indians by Angela Medearis.
Brown Bear, Brown Bear, What Do You See? by Bill Martin/Eric Carle.
When I Was Young in the Mountains by Cynthia Rylant.
In A People House by Theo LeSeig.

Books Serena Has Read Independently:
The Cat in the Hat by Dr. Seuss.
The Berenstains' B Book by the Berenstains.
Green Eggs and Ham by Dr. Seuss.
Mrs.Wishy-washy.
Brown Bear, Brown Bear, What Do You See? by Bill Martin/Eric Carle.
My Journal by Serena Jones.
The Pumpkin Book by Serena Jones.
The Power Ranger Book by Serena Jones.
The Numbers Book by Serena Jones.
The Two Book by Serena Jones.
The To Book by Serena Jones.
The Four Book by Serena Jones.

Portfolio Information:
Serena's portfolio contains all of the projects she worked on this semester. She wanted to include everything and she requested that it all be in order. She chose most items because she liked them. Serena said she liked reading the books she made and she enjoyed playing the games. She wanted to make more concentration cards but we ran out of time.

Summary:
I really enjoyed working with Serena this semester. She is very cooperative and responsive. She showed enthusiasm in each project we undertook. She brought new and wonderful ideas to the activities. She is outgoing, yet serious. She is truly an inspiration. I will miss working with Serena on Wednesdays.

Letters to Teachers

In preparation for their last visit, my students each write a brief thank-you note to their classroom teachers. If the teachers didn't share their children with us, there would be no program. My students also purchase and wrap coloring books and crayons for the children. They volunteer to bake an assortment of treats.

Our Final Visit

For their final visit, my students will meet with the students and some of their parents and guardians at 9:00. They arrive at 8:30 as usual to have one last half hour alone with the children. Some students and buddies review the contents of their portfolios to be sure the children remember how to play the games they've worked on all semester.

Other children tear open their presents and begin to color. It is a relaxing time. They enjoy each other's company. Right before 9:00, the first set of parents arrives. The mother is carrying a younger child in a festive bright red shirt. They sit on the rug with their child and his Salve buddy. A grandmother arrives and sits at a small desk with her grandson to peruse his work. Because of other commitments not many parents attend parents' day, but the ones who do join us seem pleased with the progress of their offspring.

The portfolios stimulate conversations and serve as a means to review accomplishments with parents and guardians. My students brag about the children's progress, and when I stop by they gladly pose for photos. One little girl flits from the rug to the bulletin board, reading everything in sight for her mom. Showing off, she revels in the excitement of having her mom and her Salve buddy in the same room at the same time.

Through this parents' day, my students gain experience with parent conferences. They learn to discuss a child's progress by sharing qualitative and anecdotal information rather than test results. Through conversations, they also gain a better understanding of parent-child relationships and the environmental circumstances that some of the parents and guardians experience.

When the children eventually line up to go to art class, I hear a few tiny voices say, "I'm going to miss you." Several of my students cry. Later they tell me, "We felt like losers but that's OK."

Sandy, who was lucky enough to have her buddy's entire family come to visit, writes in her weekly Sullivan Report:

> The best part of the day for me was when Pat's parents went on about how Pat loved working with me and every Wednesday night at the dinner table he would tell them everything we did. They said that he talked about me so much that they had to come to school to meet me.

Trisha writes about her meeting with Darlene's mom:

> Mrs. N told me all the wonderful things Darlene says about me at home. Apparently she picks out an outfit every Tuesday night just for me, something she thinks I would like.

Liane finishes her Sullivan Report with the following:

> I was so sad when I left. He hugged me about seven times. I have really become attached to this little boy. I hope we can return to Sullivan next semester. I would love to work with him again.

As we approach the end of the semester, my students become more interested in continuing our work through the spring. During our last week of classes I take a poll to determine how many would be willing to devote one hour each Wednesday morning next semester. Although it's too early for them to know all their commitments for spring, almost half the class is willing to do so. At Sullivan, the teachers believe it would be good for the relationships to continue, and the principal is thrilled. It will be the first time we will work with the first graders for an entire year. We'll see.

The Final Exams

On the take-home final exam I ask my students what advice they would offer to someone who wanted to teach a child to read, what they feel they have taught their buddies, and what their buddies have taught them. Since it is the first time that most of my students have worked in an at-risk school, I want to know what they have learned from this experience and what they find effective when working with children in this environment. Also, I want them to analyze what they have learned about themselves as teachers and people.

In their exams some offer specific technical advice and employ educational jargon. Overall, however, subtle advice of a more thoughtful nature emerges—advice that I consider indicative of practitioners who will reach beyond programs and teach children. They write with authentic voices. They don't regurgitate information but instead communicate from the stance of experience. Here are parts of the exams written by Jenna, Colleen, Mattie, and AnnMarie.

Jenna

Jenna is forthright in her advice to someone who is about to teach reading for the first time. She writes:

> Forget about how you were taught to read. Be open-minded. There is no best way to teach a child to read. I was taught with a basal reader and direct teaching. When I first met my buddy I thought that was the way he should be taught. I was blind to other ways. Look closely at your child and decide which method the child will benefit from when he is in the beginning stages of reading.
>
> Be patient with the child because even though the child seems that he is not trying, chances are he really is but he just cannot get the answer. As a teacher you need to understand that and be there when the child needs help. When a student is having trouble, you need to let him know it is OK to make mistakes because everyone is not perfect. That is how we improve.

> Children need to see that you are motivated. You need to have
> a positive attitude when teaching a child to read because at times it
> is frustrating. You cannot rush through teaching a child to read. It
> takes time and a lot of positive reinforcement.

Throughout the semester Jenna questioned her past experiences in learning to read; lessons had been teacher-directed and Jenna had not had a choice. In contrast with these experiences, she has shown sensitivity to her buddy's needs. She has avoided dictated instruction. As a result, she feels that she has positively affected Mic's learning:

> I feel I have taught my buddy to read. We worked with the whole
> language approach and I emphasized using the four cues. I also taught
> my buddy word-family groups, sight words, and color words. I have
> built his self-confidence and he feels he can accomplish anything he
> comes across. He is more determined and motivated than before; you
> can see this in his attitude. The important thing is he set a goal at the
> beginning that he wanted to read me a book by himself and he did.

In turn, Jenna appreciates what Mic has taught her about risk-taking and perseverance. Throughout the semester Mic has remained focused and, at such a young age, has been able to help Jenna gain confidence in herself as a teacher. During their first visit together, when Jenna acted a little unsure about her lesson, Mic even said, "Don't be nervous." Jenna writes:

> My buddy has taught me to be understanding and have patience. He
> has shown me to always give 100% and keep trying even though
> you may not get the right answer. Trying is just as good. Always set
> reachable goals for yourself and never give up until they have been
> accomplished to your satisfaction. Don't settle for less than the best.

Jenna also explains how much fun she has had working with Mic. When she was learning to read, she didn't have fun. There was no communication among students in her classes, and so this present opportunity to incorporate games and read for pleasure with Mic has helped her to realize that learning to read can and should be fun.

Jenna also comments on her impressions of an at-risk environment:

> I feel my buddy is not an at-risk child but I have seen at-risk children
> in my buddy's classroom. As adults, the attention we give them is
> effective in itself. They become close to their Salve buddies and work
> harder to make their Salve buddies proud. My views about at-risk
> children have not changed because I never stopped believing in
> them and I never will.

Jenna held no preconceived ideas that children attending at-risk schools were less able than children in schools not labeled at-risk. Jenna has remained positive throughout the semester.

Taking this course and working with Mic have increased not only her confidence but her outlook as a teacher:

> I have learned that I cannot judge children from the outside. I need to get to know them as people, not just children in my class. I need to give children a chance to express themselves and to be themselves. Judging children from their school work alone is just like judging a book by its cover. It should not be done.
>
> Children can make a difference in your life whether it is directly or indirectly. I have grown to like working with the first grade. I was a little nervous but I conquered my fear by this wonderful experience.

During the semester my students learn a number of reading strategies that they can use with their buddies. Jenna's teachers never taught her these strategies when she attended elementary school. For Jenna, an understanding of the reading process became evident for the first time. She talks about her discoveries:

> When I was young I never used the whole text, I just memorized words. There is just so much more meaning when you use the context. I was always just pointing, and if I couldn't say the word then forget it. I never really read to understand and comprehend, I read to decode.
>
> This class doesn't just pertain to my buddy—it pertains to me too. Now when I read, I really use metacognitive strategies. Do I have to go back to reread? Do I understand? Do I know what the author's saying?

Each year I have students like Jenna who, once they gain a full understanding of the reading process, wean themselves from a more traditional teacher-centered approach to one where they value a child-centered approach. Because they teach once a week with a reflection period in between, they have time to try newer approaches and think about their discoveries. Jenna leaves this course with a new philosophy that has helped Mic and will positively affect her future students.

Colleen

Colleen, who taught José, offers her advice about teaching reading:

> Assume nothing. I went into Sullivan expecting José to know a great deal more than he did. Find out about the child first. Then let the child progress at his own pace. Read things that the child enjoys. Don't depend too heavily on letters and the alphabet right away.

Give the child themes. Show the child that reading is like talking and the main purpose is to communicate. Let the child look through books and see that there are things on the page that mean something. When it is time to begin with letters start with his name, your name, his friends' and family's names. Because that is what words are; they are names. Don't pressure and don't immediately correct every mistake that he makes. Let the child explore and feel around a little before jumping right into reading.

At the beginning of the semester, Colleen was petrified to be working with an ESL student. She had only studied French and felt totally unprepared. She struggled for a month before she discovered that meaning, rather than isolated skills, is central—especially with second language students. She has learned to work from themes and whole text.

Like Jenna, Colleen believes she has made a difference in her buddy's life:

I taught my buddy what reading is about. I have taught him all the neat things that books can do. He wants to read. He likes books and stories and pictures. He likes to write. He understands that there is a code to reading and he is beginning to crack it! He is beginning to read and takes great pride in that fact.

I have helped José by believing in him. I was genuinely thrilled with every step he made and I let him know that. I wouldn't let him give up, but I never overworked or burdened him. He needs a lot of time and a lot of practice and I gave that to him while we were together. I think the buddies understood that we were there for only them and that we wanted them to do the best they could. Language must be scary and confusing for him and I think that I helped take away some of the "scariness" about books. I gave José a glimpse of literacy.

José and the other children have taught Colleen about working in an at-risk environment. She continues:

When I first went to Sullivan I felt so bad for the kids. My views have definitely changed. I learned not to pity them. I don't know what I thought before this course. I guess that was my fault, I didn't think of these kids. But the more I got to know them, I saw that at-risk children are children. They giggle and laugh and cry and watch Power Rangers and are waiting for Santa just like any other kids. They are exactly like we were. They play the same games I played! When the kids came to Salve we ran around and climbed trees. No matter where someone lives, everyone starts off as a little kid.

It's very sad to think that their lives might only get harder. I'm glad that I had a chance to protect José's little smile for a while. I wish at-risk environments didn't exist but I can't think of a more challenging and satisfying type of environment to teach in when I am older. I've never felt more needed in my entire life since I started my relationship with the children at Sullivan School.

I think teachers have the greatest potential to change and help a child's life. I want to be needed, I want to make change, and I want to help. At-risk children are a challenge and at times very frustrating and depressing, but when José looked up at me and said " I love you Colleen," I knew how much he needed me. José taught me patience, faith, understanding, and the importance of trust.

Many of my students had never been exposed to at-risk children. They are used to attending school where children have money and are considered "good students." A number of my students have expressed how working at Sullivan has changed their views.

Colleen completes her exam by describing what she has learned about herself through this experience. She writes:

I'm flexible and adaptable. I am also very patient and have gained confidence in my abilities to teach through my time at Sullivan. I have a big heart. It's almost a little too big at times! However, I think that is so important for a teacher to possess. I also love kids and more importantly I respect kids. I am going to be a good teacher.

Mattie

Mattie, who has viewed this semester from the perspective of a college graduate, mother, and African American, offers her suggestions to those who would teach reading:

Respect the child. Believe that each child wants to learn. Appreciate the differences each child brings to the learning experience and build on these differences. Use these differences as positives. Build the self-confidence of the child. Set the standards high because it comes across that you think they can do it. Form a partnership with the child. Find topics that are of particular interest to the child. Read children's literature as much, as often, and in as many different formats as possible. Talk to teachers and other experts in the field for ideas and support.

We don't have many older students like Mattie who return to the university to follow our undergraduate methods courses. Those who do, however, bring a broader knowledge of life that helps them to interpret experiences with a mature understanding. Although Mattie has worked primarily with her buddy, she has observed much of what has happened in the classroom between her classmates and their buddies. She learns from everyone in the environment. She summarizes her thoughts:

I have seen how children bring all of their life experiences with them into the school environment. I have learned that sometimes things look and sound good on paper but they don't necessarily work when put into practice.

I learned that all children are capable of learning. A teacher/
friend/buddy's confidence in the child's ability has a positive effect
on the child as an individual. The most effective tools are patience
and a genuine concern for the child.

The term *at-risk* has bothered Mattie from the beginning of this
course. She is sensitive to the impact that prejudice places on individuals. Although her buddy is one of the most advanced in the class, she
worries:

> I think about the fact that these children are considered at-risk. I
> look at my buddy and see how much she can do, and then I think
> about how she can be held back by so many other things that don't
> have anything to do with how smart she is or whether or not she is
> capable of doing the work. She has a good family life but other fac-
> tors could affect her, like drugs in the community or she could get
> hit by a stray bullet. I wonder whether she'll really make it. She has
> a very good chance of not.
>
> People are going to look at her and they're going to see at-risk.
> When people do see what she knows they are going to be surprised,
> but there are going to be a lot of people who are not going to give
> her a chance because they don't think she can do it. Although peo-
> ple don't mean it, they can be a little patronizing and set standards
> for her that might not be as high.

Because of Mattie's observations about Serena, I think she will fight
even harder to eliminate prejudice. She continues:

> Everybody has preconceived notions. It's very easy to stereotype
> people. When you find out you've done this it startles you because
> you never think that you would think a certain way or expect a
> certain thing. I remember when I first went in to Sullivan I thought
> "Oh this is at-risk." Then I got Serena and I said to myself, "Well
> that's what you get for that thought. You get Serena who does
> so well." She made me realize you have to take children as in-
> dividuals.
>
> My views on at-risk children have not changed. The same things
> that work with at-risk children benefit children in a regular class-
> room. I know these children need all the love, protection, and
> understanding that every child needs, but I understand the impor-
> tance of the school providing more intense programs and a safe envi-
> ronment for these children. It may be the only safe haven they have.

Mattie learned about herself, too, this semester:

> This semester I thought a lot more seriously about issues in school
> and how children learn. I always said I want to teach, I want to give
> to the community, I want to work. It's like this thing I always
> wanted to do. Now I'm more aware of the importance of what I say
> and do. I must do it right because it's going to make a big difference.

I am sure now that I want to be a teacher. I want to work in an at-risk environment. I have the drive and the desire.

AnnMarie

AnnMarie has been one student this semester who has really trans-lated theory into practice. She offers some of the most concrete advice to a person who might want to teach a child to read:

> Find out their interest as a foundation for your plans for each lesson. Give them choices and hands-on activities. This makes learning fun. If you are tutoring, find out from the teacher what skills the child needs to work on.
>
> Have a variety of lessons planned because you never know what type of mood or problems you're going to have with the child. Have a variety of books for the child to read for each lesson and also have lots of materials such as construction paper, tape, a glue stick, crayons, markers etc. Have a pad for yourself to write down notes to yourself about the progress of the child or if the child is having problems with a particular lesson. Keep a portfolio of the child's work so you can show the child's progress to the teacher, the parent, and the child.
>
> When you teach a lesson, you should complete the activities alongside your buddy. If I told Carl that I wanted to have him draw his favorite part in a story, I would also draw my favorite part of the story. Then we would share ideas and our pictures. We learned from each other.
>
> Children want to be heard and they want to show you what they can do. Give them that chance.

AnnMarie has worked consistently and monitored Carl's progress. She has been especially concerned about her buddy. At one point during the semester, I asked her what she had learned about herself by working with her buddy. She replied, "That's a tough question. I don't know. I've been so worried about him that I haven't thought about myself." On her exam she comments:

> I see Carl as an at-risk student because of his speech. He's one of eighteen and he doesn't listen very well. If he gets bored, he's definitely hard to handle. Therefore he's really not learning. I'm kind of scared for Carl because I want him to do well. I want him to get to second grade. I know how it feels to stay back because I had to stay back in fourth grade and I wouldn't wish that on any little kid.

When AnnMarie was in fourth grade, she would never really read a book but would rely on others in her class to summarize it for her. The books were always too hard. Now she wishes someone would have said, "What's going on, why aren't you reading this book? Let's find another book for you." Because of her personal failure, she has worked very hard to ensure that Carl gained good strategies and a positive attitude toward reading. She was very careful not to frustrate him or get annoyed with him. She gave him constant support.

For a student who was reticent in September, AnnMarie has flourished and expresses what she has learned about herself:

> I love to make a difference in people's lives—especially those who need it. I have built confidence in myself because I know that if I started to break or show Carl that I was getting frustrated with him, he would have just eaten me alive! Now I prepare myself and I believe I can teach.

Each year the take-home final allows my students the time to reflect, analyze, and write about their idiosyncratic experiences. They discover what they have learned, and it is always more than how to teach reading and writing. It also helps them to gain an appreciation of the necessity, importance, and power of self-evaluation. As one student commented:

> This take-home part of the final exam has given me an opportunity to look back on the whole experience and smile. Keep it. I can't say that about everything I've done this semester in my courses. Take it as a big compliment.

Reflections

This semester has been satisfying—both the children and the university students have learned a lot together. Through the children's work with their Salve buddies, they can now identify and recite the alphabet, print their names, and construct individual dictionaries. They dictate and illustrate books that reflect their interests and imagination. They use invented spelling to tell stories about their pets and friends. They associate words with pictures and use both phonics and sentence structure to identify unknown words. They've increased their sight vocabulary and learned to refer to printed materials in the classroom to help them with their spelling. They can read simple books. Above all, they like reading and writing.

The children also learned that they can trust and depend on the university students to support them in their efforts. These friends don't criticize their mistakes but provide a patient ear and a smile each week. The children have had the chance to share their lives with their Salve buddies, and in return they have learned about the lives of very literate people. They visited the university and gained an understanding of the possibilities that could await any of them. The children befriended role models who would listen to them and answer their questions.

The children weren't the only ones who learned this semester. My students learned about a whole new system of teaching reading and writing. The phonics workbooks, ditto sheets, and basal reader lessons they grew up with were not available to them now as sources of instruction. Instead, they created lessons around children's literature books, constructed language experience stories, and designed games that reinforced letter recognition and sight words. They've let the children explore their own reading and writing, and they have praised them for their attempts without correcting every mistake. My students grew to believe in the concept of emergent literacy. Participating in whole language classrooms for an extended period of time allowed them to break from their stereotypical memories of elementary school and discover the value of a child-centered philosophy. They learned not to prejudge but rather to listen to children's fears, interests, and perceptions of their abilities. They are now able to encourage children to reveal what they need to know to become better readers and writers.

Throughout the semester my students have recorded their reactions to each class, written and reflected upon all reading assignments, and completed weekly Sullivan Reports. They've dated and kept all their work in their manila folders. Toward the end of the semester they reflected upon the contents of these folders to complete their final exams and final Sullivan Reports. As a result of this process, they've learned the importance of accurate record-keeping and how to translate and use data to measure their own as well as the children's progress.

Sharing our portfolios has also taught us some valuable lessons. It has linked me, my students, the children, and their families. When I modeled for my students how I had constructed my own portfolio, I introduced them to the process of saving artifacts that reflect beliefs, habits, and attitudes about reading, writing, learning, and life. They also got to know me as a person rather than a professor, and they realized how much we have in common. When they shared their portfolios with each other and the children, they reviewed their strengths as students, readers, writers, and people.

When we return from Christmas break, I will have the privilege of working with these same university students throughout the second semester. We will use the collections in their portfolios as topics of exploration as we delve into the teaching of the writing process. They will discover how to interpret these collections and translate them into major pieces of writing.

This semester has also provided the essential field experience that has helped my students to understand America's shifting ethnicity. Minority children comprise about 40 percent of the Sullivan School population. For many of my students it was the first time they had the opportunity to work with children whose backgrounds and upbringing differed substantially from their own. Each week following our session with the children, when teachers and social service personnel from the school talked with my students, they raised my students' consciousness of some of the problems and obstacles that these children face. It also helped my students to meet some of the parents. Contrary to many of the general stories my students had heard about the difficult home lives of at-risk children, these parents supported the school's efforts, worked faithfully with their children, and wanted them to succeed. At the end of the semester, one of my students who graduated from a small, private high school wrote about how her introduction to an at-risk environment affected her:

> When you don't know much about something you tend to have falsified views. I realize now that the children that we worked with are very smart people, but they need the family environment and the proper teachers in order to be given the chance to show what they can learn. . . . It has been really sad and frustrating to hear of students that haven't had the "perks" that I have had in my life. It only makes me want to teach more, especially students like this. . . . The children in this type of environment have big hearts and the potential to overcome what they have against them.

All the lessons we learned this semester could not have happened if we didn't have time for sustained, in-depth, and focused exploration in a genuine, purposeful teaching situation. Working one-on-one enabled my students to form a bond with the children. Simultaneously or in syncopation my students and the children failed, doubted their abilities, then rebounded to new heights. Each week their friendships helped my students to develop as teachers and the children to develop as readers and writers. They gave each other the gift of confidence.

Sustained exploration also helped my students to make decisions about the teaching profession. Although the majority of my students were fairly confident about their choice to become teachers, a few needed this time to secure that decision. Others determined which grade levels they would like to teach and whether or not they would like to pursue a double major in elementary and special education. As happens each year, some of my students found the teaching of reading so interesting that they decided to pursue it further in graduate school.

My students have learned that teaching is hard but vitally important work. As Lucy Calkins (1994) says:

> What an awesome responsibility this is knowing our teaching matters this much . . . I believe that when we recognize how much our teaching matters we become activists defending with all our might our right to teach wisely and well. (516)

There could never be enough journal-writes, discussions, or exams to capture all the learning that transpired this semester. But participating in the Sullivan experience brought us all closer to an understanding of what Tom Newkirk (1992) refers to as the enigma of instinct, the inner game, "the moment-by-moment decision-making of the skilled teacher" (115). He explains that the information that beginning teachers in methods courses seek cannot "be reduced to general statements of principle or philosophy. This skill is contextual, personal, particular, local; it can be revealed but not abstractly defined" (117).

Our Sullivan School partnership provides us with an environment to begin to develop this instinct. This semester we all had the time and vested interest to improve the literacy skills of children we cared for, even loved. We had a safe, supportive community—what Lucy Calkins (1990) describes as "shoulders to stand on"—as we struggled to learn about teaching. We have translated abstract book knowledge into reality—an experience for which we are all grateful.

Chapter Eight

Concrete Tutoring Advice

Readers interested in our program and its development over the past five years might want to start a tutoring program in their community. Working together, my students and I have compiled a list of the most difficult situations and/or obstacles they encountered while tutoring their buddies and how we handled them. Here we directly offer tutors some helpful strategies, suggestions, and materials to ease them into their first experience with beginning readers and writers.

Prepare for the Initial Visit

Purchase a tote bag to reserve for tutoring. Once it is stocked, you can grab it on your way out the door and know that you will have everything you need when you get to your assignment. Each week, you can also place your lesson plan in a folder in the front of this bag along with the children's literature books, extension activities, and games you create. It is best to stock the bag with at least the following items:

8" x 11" white paper

Lined writing pads

A package of colored construction paper

Magic markers

Crayons

Pencils

Several manila folders

A package of 3" x 5" cards

Scissors

A glue stick

A stapler

A Dolch Word List (to remind you of the most frequent words used by beginning readers)

Upper- and Lowercase Alphabet Cards (you can make these yourself)

Plastic Alphabet Letters (magnetic letters work well if the class has a magnetic board, a file cabinet, or even a small cookie sheet)

A small notepad (to record weekly observations)

In addition, find a shoe box to leave with your child. It will serve as a safe place to store work from session to session. This work can be reviewed periodically and also be transferred to a portfolio as it progresses. It's helpful if you can determine ahead of time whom you will be working with and what observations the classroom teacher has made about his or her skills, abilities, interests, behaviors or attitudes. (If it is early in the year, teachers may not have this information yet.) It is also helpful to have an idea about what the teacher wishes to accomplish with the children during the year. This will help you to coordinate your lessons with the expectations the teacher holds for the children. This also provides continuity for the child.

Complete an Initial Assessment

It's only natural to feel a little anxious and excited before your first visit with your buddy. Many of my students felt this was the biggest obstacle to overcome. My students worried about their lack of experience and that they might be expected to teach these children to read and write before our course was over. Don't place undue stress upon yourself. You will find a wide discrepancy among the abilities of beginning readers and writers and among the children's learning styles and paces. My students suggest that during your first visit, you try to relax and just talk with your buddy. Begin by telling the child that you are there to help him with his reading and writing and that you will be working with him every week. It is best not to frighten the child with a series of tests. Begin gently.

Create name tags together, each printing your name on a tag. This allows you to assess whether or not the child knows how to spell his name and if he uses capital and lowercase letters. If the child can't print his name, print it for him, telling him the letters as you write.

Show the child some of the materials you have in the tote bag and focus upon designing a shoe box to hold her work. Young children like hands-on activities and this challenge usually interests them. In the process, you can review the colors of the construction paper in the pack and assess which colors the child knows. One warning—don't bring glitter. One of my students learned that although children love glitter, it can become the focal point of the entire visit if the child uses it with gusto and spreads it liberally. While the child decorates her box, you can ask some informal questions about whether or not he likes to read, if he has any favorite stories, and what he likes to do after school and on the weekends. Often children offer information about books they have at home, if they are read to, if they have brothers or sisters, and they describe their vacations and pets.

You can do a quick assessment of a child's alphabet knowledge by asking him to recite the alphabet, identify letters on the alphabet cards you have prepared, or write the alphabet on a sheet of paper. Notice if the child uses environmental print as a helping tool, and whether he uses upper- and lowercase letters.

You can do a quick assessment of a child's knowledge of numbers by simply asking her to write the numbers she knows. Number words can be used later for games and the construction of books.

You can also assess knowledge of letters, numbers, colors, and shapes in a nonthreatening manner by reading and discussing some of the children's literature books that my students recommend. The list can be found on page 109.

Come prepared to get an initial assessment of a child's reading level. Bring a variety of books—including picture books, books with one word on a page, patterned books, and books with a simple story line. Spread the books on the child's desk and let him choose the book he wants. If he chooses one he cannot read, read it to him, or let him "read" it by using the pictures as clues. If either situation doesn't work, have him continue to select books until he finds one he feels confident with. In many cases, the child will not be able to read any books.

If a child selects a simple book that she can read, keep track of her sight words and also note words she has difficulty with. See if she uses picture clues, background knowledge, syntax, or semantics to decode unknown words. Note any strategies the child reveals during a session. For example, a child might reread a sentence if it doesn't make sense, decode by looking for smaller words within multisyllabic words, or return to the text to help sequence a story. Allowing the child to select the books she wants to read also helps you to determine her interests, her ability to make choices, and her ability to describe why she has made her selection.

If the child doesn't find a book he can read, you should choose a picture book, turning the pages and letting the child tell the story in his own words. This will give you an idea about his background knowledge and the range of his vocabulary.

Also bring several books with good story lines to read to your child. Encourage her to make predictions about upcoming events. Show her the cover of the book and ask what she thinks it will be about. Stop periodically throughout the book to prove or disprove her predictions and to set new predictions. When she completes the book, ask her to retell the story in her own words. If she wants to read along at any time, encourage her to do so.

To gain a quick assessment of a child's writing ability, give him a piece of paper and have him draw his favorite part of the story. Ask him to write a word or sentence about it below the illustration. If he feels comfortable, let him write a brief story with one sentence on each page. He can later illustrate the sentences. For some children, it will be easier to draw first and write sentences later. You could also ask him to write a list of any words he knows.

You might not feel comfortable with your ability to accomplish all or any of these screening procedures, but my students say it really is a trial-and-error experience. If the material appears too easy for the child, increase the difficulty. If the child seems agitated, disinterested, or frustrated, the material may be too hard.

Even if you have an extremely cooperative child with extraordinary capabilities, it will be impossible to complete all of the above assessments at the first meeting. Don't even try. However, keep these ideas in mind for future sessions while you approximate your child's reading and writing levels.

Monitor Progress

Date everything. As tutoring progresses, it becomes more difficult to keep track of which accomplishments took place each week. It's a simple but crucial task. Although my students didn't identify monitoring a child's progress as a difficult task, they agree that it must begin at the initial visit. Always bring a small notepad and write your observations as your lesson progresses. If your child tells you she likes butterflies or that her favorite TV show is "Barney," jot yourself a note. Plan to incorporate those topics into future lessons. When you flip through your alphabet cards or work with numerals, keep track of the letters and numbers she knows and those she has difficulty with.

Design a system that helps your child to keep track of his own progress. One way is to create a list of all the books you read together.

Some of my students have generated computer-decorated booklists entitled "Books We Have Read"; others have constructed special journals with the same title. Others drew trees on posters—for each book, the child wrote the title on a leaf and placed it on the tree. Others have made bookworms, adding a segment of the worm's body for each title read. Children take pride in their accomplishments as they watch their booklists grow.

In addition, it is helpful to keep track of your child's sight words. You can do this with a miniature word-wall. Open a manila folder; print the letters of the alphabet across the spread; and, as your child learns a word, place that word under the appropriate letter of the alphabet. You also can create individual dictionaries, asking the children to create a page for each letter of the alphabet. As they learn new words, they list them under the appropriate letter. These personal dictionaries and word-walls can be used as references when the children write their own stories. Or you can let your child brainstorm how to keep track of all the words she knows.

Have the child keep a journal. At the end of each lesson have her write, draw, or dictate one thing that she enjoyed or learned during the lesson. Leave the decision up to the child. A shy student, a second-language student, or a student who thinks she can't write will probably begin by dictating something for you to write. It will take time for your student to gain the confidence to be able to write in her journal. It will help if you keep a journal as well and model how you write what interested you the most about the tutoring session. Just instructing a child to write in her journal is too abstract a concept for some children to comprehend.

Keep a record of each session. When you complete a tutoring session, go home and write about it. Each week my students complete a Sullivan Report in which they list what they planned to do, a summary of what actually happened during the lesson, what problems they need to address, and what they plan to do the following session as a result of this one. They keep all their reports and thus accumulate a chronological account of their own as well as their children's learning histories. These weekly reports are also valuable for constructing a summative evaluation.

After you have been working with a child for several weeks, it is also productive to construct a portfolio of his accomplishments. Let the child decide what should be transferred from his box to the portfolio. This gives him the chance to discuss all the books he has read, review his sight vocabulary, reread the books he has written, and play the games that have motivated him to keep on task throughout the tutoring. A portfolio also serves as a means for the child to share his knowledge and skills with his teacher, peers, and his parents or guardians when they come to visit the school.

Prepare a Weekly Plan

One area that my students found difficult was weekly planning. Very often with young children, especially those with short attention spans, it is advisable to overplan and prepare a variety of lessons. One of my students explained that her child could not focus on one activity for more than ten minutes at a time. So for her hour and fifteen minutes, she had to prepare at least six or seven different lessons that she could draw upon.

I advise my students to outline their lessons and collect the books and materials necessary to implement them. Include in your weekly plan some time to read to your child. On page 109 my students provide a list of books they found helpful for read-alouds, echo, and choral reading. Also give your child a chance to read to you each week.

Plan to engage the child in a writing activity. Most children like to write their own books that stem from personal experience or spin off from a story you just read.

Model a strategy or reinforce a skill each week. This might be a review of the alphabet, a game that teaches number words, or an explanation of how word families work. The key is to keep the lessons child-centered, keep track of your child's progress, and plan your next lessons based upon what you learn about your child each week.

One problem that arose with my students' weekly planning was the fact that children would know something one week and not the next. Just when they thought they could move on with their plans, they had to step back. Respond to the children. If it means repeating last week's lesson again, do it. Children need lots of practice. One of my students advises that you begin each lesson with a quick review of what you did the previous session. This boosts self-confidence and helps the child to see that she knows something. Children like to reread books. Let them. Don't feel you aren't making progress. Many of my students reported that their children read the same book every week before they'd move on to new work.

Try new approaches to reinforce the same skill. Integrate as many hands-on activities and games as possible. Play concentration or word bingo to reinforce such things as basic sight vocabulary, alphabet knowledge, and number words.

My students didn't find it difficult to write child-centered plans, but they did find it difficult when their plans didn't always work out for them. If lessons don't go as you hope, you should not feel like you failed. Be sure to ask yourself why things didn't go as planned and modify your lesson for the next visit. Maybe the books you brought or the activities you planned were too difficult or didn't interest the child. Maybe you didn't activate background knowledge before trying to teach a new concept. Maybe you didn't model what you wanted the child to do and he got confused or frustrated.

Above all, realize that sometimes your lack of success is a result of influences beyond your control. Maybe your child had a difficult morning before coming to school, or didn't have a good breakfast, or didn't get enough rest. Maybe she's got a cold and feels terrible. Remain positive. As long as your plans relate directly to the interests and the developing abilities of your child, know that next time your child should respond.

Motivate the Child to Reduce Behavior Problems and Improve Attitudes

Probably one of the most difficult challenges my students faced was getting their children motivated enough to pay attention and remain focused on the task at hand. They feel confident with what they plan to teach, but often they aren't able to execute their plans because their children won't participate.

My students' first piece of advice to new tutors is to direct lessons to the child's interest. One child this semester really liked bridges. My student found all the books she could on bridges and got him interested in reading because of this. She also kept track of the books he read by creating a poster with a bridge on it. She drew cars on individual sheets of paper, and as they read each book he would write the title and author on a car and glue it to the poster.

My students advise that you remain firm yet flexible. The children will sometimes try to avoid work by jumping up from their chairs and wandering around the room. They will inspect what others are doing or want to share everything they create with their classroom teacher and all the other children. You have to let them know that you are there to help them learn, you enjoy working with them, and you are proud of what they can do. Tell them you are as excited about their work as they are, but that they need to remain in their seat or work area. When they have accomplished some of their work, reward them. Take a break and let the children go to the bathroom or get a drink of water. Take a tour of the classroom and let them explain what goes on there during the week when you are not there, or let them share what they have done with a peer.

My students found that choice is a very effective method to motivate children. Many of my students bring a list of all they want to accomplish with the children that day and begin the lesson by sharing the list. They let the children decide the order in which they will proceed. Some choose to read, others want to start with a game, some want to write a book. Another student wrote all her activities for the day on slips of paper and placed them in a bag. She called this her "bag of tricks." Her buddy loved reaching into the bag to select what they would do. It was always a surprise. Choice gives children power and gets them excited to work hard.

Toward the end of the session, let your child choose some activity or game he would like to play. Often the child wants to reread a book or play a game from that day's lesson or from previous lessons. This is easy if all materials, books, and games are readily available in his shoe box or your tote bag.

Not all children are motivated intrinsically. Some need to be rewarded with stickers! We discuss this before we begin the semester. If you are in a tutoring situation with other tutors working alongside you, you have to make a group decision about rewards. We limit our rewards to stickers or motivational charts. No presents, toys, or food are allowed. Some of my students designed game boards that ran from start to finish. After their buddies completed a book or activity, they would be allowed to place a sticker on the game board. Others awarded stickers directly on good papers, journals, or onto the children's shirts. Often the children marched proudly out to their art or gym classes wearing colorful and fragrant stickers of pumpkins, animals, or unicorns.

Sometimes shy children or children who are easily distracted by what others are doing around them become motivated to work if they can learn alongside a peer. Two of my students found it valuable to plan their weekly lessons together and construct activities that the children could jointly accomplish. This took the pressure off the shy child and gave the more energetic child the chance to direct his efforts to assist his friend.

Plan lessons that address your child's learning style. One little boy did not like to be read to. He could not remain still. His tutor discovered that he liked to write books, which he later would read instead. The act of writing the book focused his attention and motivated him to become interested in reading what he wrote. From this he gained some sight vocabulary and was later more willing to be read to because he had some success with reading.

Another child loved to draw, so my student based all her lessons around art activities. Once she created a poster with a turkey on it and before the little boy could add a feather, he had to write a letter of the alphabet on it and say the letter. He also wrote his name on feathers and added them. Initially, he had great difficulty with the alphabet; this motivated him to concentrate. When he completed the bird, he added real feathers and Christmas bows to decorate the entire project. The turkey was garish beyond belief but by the end of the semester, through a variety of art activities, this little boy learned half the letters of the alphabet.

Themes help to motivate some children, especially if you can center them around the child's interests. For José, dinosaurs enticed him to participate in a lesson for the first time. Themes help to unify a lesson—even though you might switch activities, the background information remains the same. Themes build concepts and reinforce sight vocabulary.

Pacing is crucial. Do not rush your child to the point that you frustrate her. Give her time to digest what you are doing. On the other hand, don't dwell on a lesson that drags. If you sense that your child is bored, you can be sure that this will lead to distraction and even behavior problems. You will be able to sense what is right for your child after only a few visits.

One last thing to think about is feedback. In a one-on-one situation, it is very easy to ensure that your child is getting attention and feedback. Be sure, however, that your feedback is content-oriented. It is easy to say "nice job" and "good work," but after a while these phrases lose their effectiveness. It is more encouraging to hear such things as, "I like the way you read that page. When you didn't know that word, you looked at the pictures to help you decide what was going on in the story." This will help your child realize not only that you approve of his performance, but the reason why you approve.

If your child makes mistakes, don't feel that you must correct each and every one of them. Too much negative feedback will certainly turn a child off to reading and writing. My students found it difficult to overlook mistakes or miscues, especially at the beginning of the semester. But as they worked with the children, they realized that they should concentrate on meaning and communication first. As one student says, "Don't point out every problem, point out EVERY positive thing. If a child spells the word *ball* as *bghfc* say, "Good job, you got the first letter! How did you do that? Let's do the same thing to get the rest of the letters!"

When you do make corrections, focus on one or two main issues, words, or strategies per visit. When you think about all the things these young children need to learn about reading and writing, the list is overwhelming. Don't try to accomplish everything at once. You and the child will be happier for it.

Last Minute Suggestions

Two of my students offer you some last minute suggestions. Colleen begins:

> Talk to your child. If you don't know your child, you can't teach him. Also talk to your friends, classmates, and especially teachers. My classmates were constantly thinking of ways to do a better job. We'd talk and read and get great ideas from each other. Language is communication, so communication is essential to teach language.

Jenna adds:

> Become confident in yourself that you can accomplish anything you set your mind to. Keep an open mind to new ideas and suggestions because that will make a difference. Do not judge children by their appearances. It is what's inside that counts. The most important advice I leave you is to be happy and smile. When the children see that smile and happiness, they become motivated to learn.

Books for Beginning Readers

Besides offering helpful suggestions, my students want to share with you some of the books they read to the children during the semester (see pages 109–116). We have tried to place them into categories, but many do belong to more than one category.

Remember, when you first tutor it will be a learning process for both of you. Many of my students have told me that it is one of the most rewarding experiences they have encountered. You can expect the same. My students and I wish you well in your first endeavors.

Chapter Nine

Outreach Efforts: Building New Links

10/31/90   I feel that Morris has really come a long way and at the end of the semester I will hate to have to say "Have a nice life." I just can't do that. It's weird.

When Karen wrote this in one of her class reactions several years ago, I couldn't forget it. I felt the same. She wanted to continue her work at Sullivan and so did I. We knew there was more we could do. We needed to develop the means to keep our collaboration going.

Senior Partnership

Although it was impossible to create a course that would permit the juniors to continue their work at Sullivan the following semester, we did design a course called "Senior Partnership." It began in January of 1991 and has continued every spring semester since. It originally focused on Sullivan School, but has also branched out to serve children in a number of other schools and community service agencies.

The course harnesses the talent and energy of seniors who have completed student teaching. It enables them to design, implement, and evaluate semester-long projects that aim to enhance the literacy and skills of school children. The choice of the site, project, and whether or not they wish to work individually or in teams is left to the seniors.

At the beginning of the semester, the seniors meet with local teachers and community workers who agree to participate in the Senior Partnership program. Together they brainstorm projects and coordinate schedules. The teachers and community workers lend their classrooms, students, and, if asked, their suggestions and feedback. They are not responsible for supervising or grading my students but act more as mentors and friends. Everyone, including my students, donates supplies to ensure program success. In addition, several federal grants have enabled us to enhance our library collections and supplies.

A sampling of the types of projects the seniors have designed and implemented over the last five years follows:

- Teaching ESL to high school Vietnamese and Italian students
- Assisting an ESL teacher in elementary grades at two elementary schools
- Conducting writers' workshops with third and fourth graders
- Conducting story hours at the Newport Public Library
- Teaching upper-elementary students to conduct read-alouds to primary students
- Teaching poetry and literature units to fifth graders
- Teaching units on the community to second graders
- Initiating a Big Buddies program at Sullivan School
- Initiating an after-school enrichment program dealing with multiculturalism
- Introducing enrichment math programs
- Assisting in the Salvation Army After-School Program
- Investigating grant writing and writing a grant to support a children's conference on campus
- Mentoring junior education majors during field experiences dealing with integrated thematic units
- Providing individual instruction for gifted and special-needs students
- Directing and acting in an annual school play at a local school
- Supervising after-school sessions at a community center
- Working in conjunction with a local animal shelter to teach children information about pets and their care
- Assisting reading specialists
- Designing curriculum and conducting environmental tours related to the historic Rose Island Lighthouse Foundation
- Conducting Book Talks in conjunction with a children's book publishing company

In addition to working in the field, the seniors who participate in the Senior Partnership course attend a weekly seminar on campus to discuss their projects, share ideas, and offer suggestions to peers who need help with problems they encounter. Besides completing a mid-semester and final self-evaluation report, they must evaluate their experiences after each meeting with the children. Whether or not they succeed with every aspect of their project is less important than the fact that they retain their critical eye, reflect upon their teaching, and keep their sense of humor. Throughout the semester my students draft and revise articles about their projects. When their articles are finished, we bind them in a book that we reproduce for each member of the class.

Each senior is also responsible for a summative evaluation of her project at the end of the semester. Some seniors solicit evaluation letters from their classroom teachers or community workers, some audiotape interviews, and others have the elementary children write letters to express their feelings about the semester projects. Some seniors collect and submit samples of student work; others design student, teacher, and parent questionnaires, which they administer.

Probably the best part of Senior Partnership is the bond that develops among the members of the class. They have traveled together as a cohort for four years. They've labored through their methods courses and student teaching experiences; they've shared their concerns, their reading and writing, their portfolios. They know each other well, they trust each other, and feel comfortable taking risks together. Each year the chemistry among the members of Senior Partnership changes, but it is obvious that they have built coalitions and they have connected.

Senior Partnership is refreshing because my students create the curriculum according to the needs of the students in their projects. They have time to question or reflect, gain a sense of empowerment, and develop the confidence to make decisions and effect change for themselves and their students.

Big Buddies

As part of her Senior Partnership in the spring of 1991, a student named June initiated the Big Buddies program at Sullivan School. Eleven Salve students participated that semester. Each week they would spend half an hour working on academics with their elementary children and the other half hour strolling in the corridors, swinging in the school yard, or shooting baskets in the gymnasium with their buddies. Karen, the junior whose journal entry began this chapter, served as a Big Buddy that semester. During her senior year, Karen volunteered to lead the program.

In the fall of 1991, Karen rallied thirty-five university students from all majors to serve as Big Buddies at Sullivan School. Mike and the classroom teachers selected the elementary students based on their needs. Mike had his own list culled from those students whose problems required frequent visits to his office.

Karen called me periodically to keep me informed. I could trust and depend upon her to organize meetings, match buddies, and deal with the day-to-day crises that occurred. She volunteered her time generously and was quick to sense and respond to the needs of the university students.

After two semesters, I met with five of the Big Buddies for their evaluation of the program and to gather suggestions for improvement. Smiles stretched across their faces as they recounted how close they had grown to their buddies. In fact, four of the five Big Buddies had met their children not only during the school day, but also after school and on weekends.

However, the program still needed adjustments. Non-education majors felt we needed to provide more background information about working with children and using various teaching techniques. Some thought we should expand the program beyond Sullivan to the Thompson Junior High, where kids have more academic problems and start to think about dropping out. Some suggested recruitment strategies and end-of-the-year celebrations such as field trips, kite-flying days, or cookouts on campus. We brainstormed some ideas about raising funds and tapping businesses for support. We also discussed the need to involve the parents with our program and considered ways to help parents who might want to improve their own as well as their children's literacy skills.

Before we left the meeting, Karen shared a last-minute thought:

> You know, I think that for all the human services areas on campus like administration of justice, social work, nursing, psychology, and education, it should be required that everyone gives one hour a week for one semester during their four years. We're supposed to come out of here with a sense of service to others. This experience has been a very important part of my learning process. I learned more working with Morris than I learned from many of my courses.

Student Literacy Corps Tutoring and Mentoring Grants

Although Salve does not require participation in community service, many of the Big Buddies' suggestions for program improvement were realized through two new elective courses that we created. Mary

O'Brien, another member of the Elementary Education Department, and I wrote for and received two federal grants for $50,000 (Award Number P219A20011) and $30,000 (Award Number P2194A3005193) respectively to establish Student Literacy Corps Tutoring and Mentoring programs. We designed and administered two three-credit courses entitled Project S.A.L.V.E. (Students Advance Literacy through Volunteering in Education); and Project A.I.M. (Aquidneck Island Mentoring).

Project S.A.L.V.E.

This tutoring course enables university students to use their content area expertise and tutorial skills to enhance the literacy of economically and/or educationally disadvantaged children in Newport. It requires tutors to participate in a weekly two-and-a-half-hour seminar class held on campus or at an outreach center. This helps them gain the skills and confidence needed to tutor. They are required to tutor one-on-one or in small groups for a total of sixty hours per semester, which ensures that the university students consistently work with and monitor tutee progress.

The university tutors work at Sullivan Elementary School, Rogers High School, a local group home for adolescent girls, and the Martin Luther King Center, which serves youth during after-school hours. Tutors keep notebooks in which they record dates, places and times of tutoring. They separate the remainder of their notebooks with dividers labeled with the names of their tutees. After each tutoring session, they complete a journal entry as well as collect occasional samples of the tutee's work. Since the beginning of the Student Literacy Corps Tutoring Grant, university tutors majoring in American Studies, Elementary Education, Special Education, English, Anthropology, Politics, Secondary Education, Psychology, Administration of Justice, Human Resources Management, Nursing, and Sociology have shared their expertise and compassion with 167 economically and/or educationally disadvantaged children.

Project A.I.M.

Through our work with students in the Big Buddies program and our interaction with the tutors in Project S.A.L.V.E., we discovered a need not only to focus upon the children's academic achievement but in many cases to increase children's self-esteem through the use of positive role models. Frank Smith (1992) writes:

> Learning is social and developmental. We grow to be like the people we see ourselves as being like. Learning is therefore also a matter of identity, of how we see ourselves. But our identity is determined for us socially as well. We learn who we are from the way others treat us. Moreover, the learning is *vicarious*; it is not a consequence of instruction and practice but of demonstration and collaboration. We learn from the people who interest us and help us to do the things that they do. We often refer informally to people who have been significant influences on our lives—helping to make us the people we are today—as our "teachers," whether or not we met them in the classroom. (434)

Our course titled Aquidneck Island Mentoring provides training for undergraduate students from various academic departments to serve as mentors. We develop the understanding and skills necessary to work effectively with students in the areas of self-esteem, conflict resolution, self-discovery, positive thinking, cultural sensitivity, goal-setting behaviors, decision-making, problem-solving, and life-planning. The primary focus of mentoring is not on academics, although mentors will tutor children during some of their sessions. This course also requires sixty hours per semester of mentoring and a weekly seminar in which the university students share information, engage in reflective practice, and exchange promising techniques. In addition, we hold a mid-semester social night on campus for the mentors, the children, their parents/guardians, and personnel from various social service agencies. We also hold workshops for parents and field trips for the children.

Through this grant, we have been able to build links with personnel and children at the local junior high school, the Newport Public Library, the agencies served by the Department of Children and Family Services, the Salvation Army After-School Program, and the Children's Crusade, a state-wide initiative to keep children in school and off drugs. Funds from both federal grants allowed us to purchase supplies such as math manipulatives, children's literature books, computer software, dictionaries, and games. We house these at the outreach centers where they are easily accessible to our students and the children.

Our students benefit as much from their participation in the tutoring and mentoring courses as the children whom they are serving. The university students gain an understanding of the academic and social needs of economically and/or educationally disadvantaged children. Through seminars they are exposed to some of the latest teaching techniques, the problems of the school systems, and the circumstances that at-risk children must overcome. With both university and public school teachers, they analyze and discuss their questions, teaching strategies, and problems. Although they won't all become teachers, they learn that they possess the skills and desire to pursue community service again.

Our Most Recent Outreach Efforts

To this point I've only discussed some of our collaborative efforts with schools and agencies in Newport. Over the years, however, our students have completed a number of field placements and student teaching assignments with some wonderful teachers in Newport, Middletown, and Portsmouth—the three cities and towns that comprise Aquidneck Island, where Salve Regina is located. We've recently begun two new collaborative efforts that should provide new links to service teachers and children in our communities: the Aquidneck Collaborative for Education, and the Professional Development School.

Aquidneck Collaborative for Education (ACE)

We have recently formalized a collaboration among all the educators on Aquidneck Island. The Aquidneck Collaborative for Education (ACE) is designed so that all of the early childhood centers; all of the independent, parochial, private, and public elementary and secondary schools on the island; the Maher Center for special education students; and Salve Regina join forces to promote education as a community value. This collaborative provides opportunities for professional development, instructional advancement, expansion and extension of learning opportunities, sharing of facilities and resources, and communication among the educational institutions. We see that the formalization of ACE can only add to our ability to address future needs more effectively.

Professional Development School

In late November of 1994, the Rhode Island State Department of Education granted Sullivan School and Salve Regina University funds to support the planning and implementation process to develop a Professional Development School. This school will unite Sullivan, Salve Regina, parents, business and community members in a shared vision to support opportunities for the Sullivan children. Representatives from all groups will meet throughout the spring and summer to construct an exemplary model of teaching and learning in the areas of special ser-vices to students and in math and science teaching and learning. We also want to design opportunities for preservice and inservice teachers to develop their teaching abilities and to collaboratively engage in ac-tion research. This research will help them explore in a focused way what works with their students or discover if a problem can be solved by changing something in the classroom environment. In addition, we hope to explore ways to improve teacher practice and student perfor-mance. We will finally have the time to discuss our needs and to develop curriculum, programs, and opportunities that will allow us to teach and learn from each other in the future.

Each semester, new opportunities and challenges arise. I never know when I pick up the phone who will be on the other end and in what ways we at the university can help the children in the commu-nity. When I review what we have accomplished to date, it really seems like this is only the beginning of adventures yet to come.

Chapter Ten

Only the Beginning

Now when I approach the end of the Newport Bridge during my commute to school, I can't imagine not taking the left fork. We've discovered the impact and value of working side by side with the children and we can't go back to living in separate worlds. What began as an experimental semester at Sullivan School has led me and my students along a wonderful journey. This journey has clarified my thoughts about teacher education programs, literacy, and commitment to community service.

Teacher Education Programs

Critics and analysts of public education condemn much of what constitutes today's curriculum, teaching methods, and classroom environments—in short, our public school system. Clinchy (1993) writes:

> We have declared it a failure because the society those public schools were supposed to serve has changed so radically in the last 40 years that the old system and its inequities are no longer socially, morally, or intellectually acceptable. (607)

The "society" we education professors must prepare future teachers to teach differs dramatically from the one we encountered when we began to teach in elementary or secondary school classrooms. Between 1976 and 1990, the minority-group enrollment in U.S. schools has risen. The percentage of African Americans increased from 13.6 percent to 16.9 percent, the percentage of Asian Americans rose from 0.6 percent to 2.8 percent, and the percentage of Hispanic American students expanded from 6.0 percent to 10.3 percent. As a result, the percentage of European American students has dropped from 80 percent to 70 percent. (Smith 1994, 124). In addition, in 1993 more than 23 percent of America's children were living below the poverty line (Hodgkinson 1993, 620). Stevens (1992) reports that more than three hundred thousand school-age children are homeless; between one and two million are subject to abuse; and three hundred and fifty thousand newborns each year have been exposed prenatally to drugs and alcohol (18). About three million children between the ages of five and thirteen have no adult supervision after school. One study reports that these unsupervised children are twice as likely to use drugs as those children who come home to an adult who is waiting for them (Eitzen 1992, 587–588).

Not only must future teachers become accustomed to teaching children from ethnically different and sometimes troubled backgrounds, they must also prepare these children to live and work in a society that demands much more of its citizens today than ever before. Linda Darling Hammond (1993) explains that to survive and prosper today, children have to learn to engage in complex thinking; locate and make use of resources; and continuously learn new technologies, approaches, and occupations. She notes:

> The teacher's job is no longer to "cover the curriculum" but to enable diverse learners to construct their own knowledge and to develop their talents in effective and powerful ways.... This changed mission for education requires a new model for school reform, one in which policy makers shift their efforts from designing controls intended to direct the system to *developing the capacity* of schools and teachers to be responsible for student learning and responsive to student and community needs, interests, and concerns. Capacity-building requires different policy tools and different approaches to producing, sharing, and using knowledge than those traditionally used throughout this century. (754)

Goodlad (1990) agrees with Darling Hammond and adds that schools can't meet today's challenges

> simply by doing better what they have always done. Educators must rethink what education is, what schools are for and they must examine and rework the structures and practices that have always been out of sync for some students and are now revealed to be inappropriate for many. The catchword of the late 1980s for this necessary renewal was *restructuring*.

Walking the tightrope of the status quo will no longer be acceptable for our future teachers. We must empower them with the ability to create educational environments that will produce opportunities for children rather than incarcerate their intellectual potential and hope. To do this, we education professors need to restructure our education programs.

Before beginning our collaboration with Sullivan School in the fall of 1989, the students in our teacher education program observed in several classrooms, completed a two-week practicum, and culminated their education program with a semester-long student teaching experience. Unfortunately, I held a limited view of what preservice teachers needed. The students in my reading and language arts course sat in orderly rows, dutifully transcribed lecture notes, took exams, and never came in contact with children. They experienced disconnected learning. They prepared for what they might teach one day and relied upon their former K–12 teachers as role models to mold their perceptions of what teaching should be. Through my increased collaboration with the faculty from the Sullivan School and the other community outreach centers in Newport, I have learned that future teachers need and deserve much more than that.

Future teachers need to understand the "society" they will be required to teach. They will not comprehend the challenges facing them if they remain isolated on campuses being fed information through a number of discrete courses. Future teachers need to immerse themselves for a good portion of their undergraduate studies in an at-risk environment. They need to see that some children come to school hungry, grow up in homes where one or both parents are not present, and live with caretakers who often place value on areas other than education. Future teachers need to become involved enough with these children to commit a part of themselves to improving the circumstances that encompass their lives. They need to see that sustained, meaningful instruction can change not only children's attitudes but improve both their self-image and academic performance. They need to believe in the potential of every student. By working side by side with public school educators, community agency personnel, and children, university students begin to understand the commitment they must make.

Future teachers also need to develop the capacity to produce, share, and use knowledge in nontraditional ways if they are to move beyond "covering the curriculum." To do this, they must practice these nontraditional methods during their education courses and in their field experiences. We education professors need to allow our students authentic opportunities in which to construct their own knowledge, to succeed, and to fail. As Wiggins (1993) states:

> To develop a thoughtful control over performance depends not so much on learning and employing "knowledge skills" but on having

our judgment awakened and empowered through problems that demand judgment. (204)

In their book titled *Best Practice New Standards for Teaching and Learning in America's Schools* (1993) Zemelman, Daniels, and Hyde offer a synopsis of the emerging consensus of recommendations promulgated by the National Curriculum Reports (reading, science and technology, written composition, math, and social studies). The trends across these disciplines recommend less whole-class, teacher-directed instruction in which students sit passively and silently receiving information. There is less recommended "seatwork," less time spent reading basal readers, less tracking, less use of pull-out programs, and less reliance on coverage of material with an emphasis on the memorization of facts. There is also a reduced reliance on standardized tests. Instead, future directives recommend more active learning that emphasizes higher-order thinking in a collaborative atmosphere. Students should be given time, choice, and responsibility to study a smaller number of topics in order to internalize the field's methods of inquiry. Children should work in heterogeneous groups that allow them to receive special help in their regular classrooms. Teachers need to collaborate more with parents and administrators and rely more upon qualitative and anecdotal observation to monitor students' growth.

We university professors can learn some valuable lessons from the synthesis of the National Curriculum Reports. By employing many of their suggestions, I continue to move from professor-centered courses to ones that enable my students to become involved, reflective practitioners. I have reduced my need to "cover" material and have allowed my students time to explore their interactions with children and each other. Through their courses, university students conference about their progress and discuss the real problems that arise from the teaching of some very beginning readers. My students collaborate with me and the classroom teachers to devise ways to responsibly teach appropriate and meaningful lessons to their children. They do not use basals or worksheets but instead create lessons based upon children's interests. They monitor children's progress through weekly anecdotal record keeping and measure their learning without the use of tests.

On campus, my students keep journals in which they raise questions that arise from their reading and relate information to experiences past or present. This fosters meaningful discussions during class time. At the end of each class they also complete journals, which enables them to reflect on the day's topics and to ask questions that still trouble them.

I have relied less on test results and allocated a larger percentage of my students' final course grades to their performance as they work with the children and their analysis of their own learning and literacy development. Now exams count for approximately one-third of my students' grades; their completion of journal work, portfolios, and work with children contribute to my greater understanding of their learning. The exams that I do give include some open-ended response items. These allow my students the freedom to share information that they learned but I didn't already assess.

In all our outreach courses we strive to transfer the responsibility for learning and evaluation to our students. For this to work, we first spend time building community. Westheimer's (1993) definition of community summarizes the respect and trust my students must establish among themselves for any effective interaction to take place:

> We see community as a process marked by interaction and deliberation among individuals who share interests and commitment to common goals. They pursue these goals collectively, building on the distinct talents and capacities of members while valuing consensus and, at times, deferring to strongly held minority opinions. Acceptance of these opinions stems both from respect for members of the community and from a commitment to the belief that divergent ideas are often the engine of progress. Meaningful interactions among members lead to a sense of shared responsibility for both the process and its outcomes. Reflection is encouraged, and dissent is honored. (325)

As a community my students, colleagues, and I take risks to extend ourselves and our learning within the context of existing courses or to create new ones like the Student Literacy Corps to meet emerging needs. We dive into experiences and then draw theory from them. We work on common real-life projects that motivate us to help those we are working with to succeed. We encourage each other to reflect upon our experience and to suggest improvement. We do not work in a vacuum, we do not work alone, and we do not give up.

Literacy

Over the past several years through my research, reading, and interaction with my students, I have also learned to expand my understanding of and participation in literacy events. From my first encounter with the teachers and children at Sullivan School, I have continued to learn lessons about children's explorations of literacy and teachers' challenges to make their learning meaningful. Through the eyes of my students I have learned about the idiosyncratic nature of literacy as they struggled to understand and design the best path to teach their children to read and write. Denny Taylor (1989) writes:

> Acknowledging the complexity of early reading and writing develop-
> ment means that we must try to understand literacy from the child's
> perspective, and that involves disciplined, systematic observation of
> children as they work at reading and writing in and out of classroom
> settings. (186–187)

I believe this systematic observation of literacy, however, should per-
tain not only to elementary children but to university students as
well. Teacher educators must make their students read and write.
They must involve them in discussions that allow them to explore and
share insights about their own literacy development. It is only when
they truly understand literacy that they can successfully transfer this
understanding to those they will teach.

In the fall of my students' junior year, I help them begin their
exploration through the construction of portfolios. Wolf (1991)
reflects:

> Through portfolios, teaching and learning can be seen as they unfold
> and extend over time. And when the actual artifacts of teaching are
> combined with a teacher's reflections, portfolios permit us to look
> beneath the surface of the performance itself and examine the deci-
> sions that shaped a teacher's actions. . . . Portfolios are flawed as
> well, but no other method of assessment can equal them in provid-
> ing a connection to the contexts and personal histories of real teach-
> ing. (136)

The first year I introduced the concept of portfolios to my students, I
dictated the content. This resulted in uniform products that gave me
some knowledge and insight into my students' development as readers and writers, but offered them little in the area of self-exploration
and choice. Since then I have left the design of their portfolios open-
ended. As a result, I have discovered the whole of their lives. The
items they include reflect rich histories of learning and literacy and
serve as inspiration for future discussion and writing.

As we share portfolios I learn about my students, but more importantly they learn about themselves—as students, teachers, and as literate people. Each year I continue to build and share my own portfolio with my students. Our growing understanding of our strengths and
weaknesses in literacy help us shape what we need to explore to
become more complete people and educators. We have "covered" less
content in my courses, but we have explored literacy in greater depth
and with greater connectedness. My students have shared their portfolios with the children at Sullivan and, hopefully, will translate their
understanding of portfolios to their future students. Through the

power of portfolios I have learned that my students, just like elementary children, possess different strengths and weaknesses, progress at different rates, and succeed in different ways. And that is alright.

Community Service

Over the past several years as our collaboration with Sullivan and other outreach centers has grown, I have learned that an important role of teacher education programs should be to support as many young people in our community as possible. Benard (1993) states:

> Research consistently shows us that 50 to 80 percent of students with multiple risks in their lives do succeed, especially if they experience a caring school environment that conveys high expectations. (47)

At our university and probably at most colleges, there is a pool of caring and committed young people who want to share their time and expertise with children who need them. We started our commitment to the community with a pilot project in which twenty-five volunteers worked with first graders for one hour each week. We expanded, making a two-hour commitment at Sullivan each week a requirement of all juniors taking the reading and language arts course. We next designed Senior Partnership, in which seniors work not only at Sullivan but at other outreach centers that serve these children. We began a Big Buddies program, in which Salve students from all disciplines visit their little buddies for one hour per week. Through the help of two federal grants we have established a Student Literacy Corps of sophomores, juniors, and seniors who each tutor and mentor sixty hours each semester. Working in schools and community service agencies, tutors and mentors have helped students make the honor roll, appreciate their French lessons, and learn their alphabet. Children who have chips on their shoulders, have trouble with social interactions, or fight during recess now have role models to talk with and encourage them to do their best. Our next efforts lie in the Aquidneck Collaborative for Education and the Professional Development School.

Our education department is not alone in its commitment to community service. Other departments across campus offer opportunities for their students to assist a number of social service agencies. In fact, many departments support the university's mission—"to assist students to find truth, to help them become their own best selves, and to encourage them to help others become their own best selves." In recognition for such student service, the university issues a "Volunteer

Transcript" acknowledging all volunteer service that a student has contributed over his or her four years.

We hope that by participating in community service our students will learn responsible citizenship that will help them to serve their communities in the future. Some of our students might teach, others might tutor educationally and economically disadvantaged children, while some might serve on school boards. Some might become CEOs of companies and, hopefully, will encourage their employees to mentor or serve as big buddies to children or youth of greatest need.

Those of our students who have worked in the community have gained an appreciation of the hardships that today's children endure and the challenges facing teachers, and have gained some understanding of some of the latest techniques to help children learn. If for no other purpose, this knowledge and understanding will help our students when they become parents and want to help their own children. We would like to believe that even if our students do not continue their outreach efforts in the future, they have inspired and helped improve the life of at least one child during the time they have been at the university.

In all our endeavors working in collaboration with personnel from schools and community agencies on the island, there have been a number of elements common to our successes. We

- are willing to make a commitment to plans and are responsible for their operation.
- agree on common philosophies and set mutually acceptable goals.
- try to balance the needs of all involved.
- treat each other with mutual respect.
- see each other as partners.

Above all we take risks together, set high expectations, remain flexible, and allow our partnerships the time they need to develop. We keep the channels of communication open and are willing to assess and modify our direction as we see necessary.

Each semester we've caused change and we've been changed. We continue to grow and to let go. Saying good-bye only becomes difficult when you really care about someone; we're proud to say that at the end of each semester we share lots of difficult moments.

As new students enter our programs, old ones graduate to become part of the larger community of teachers and learners. Some return to Sullivan to substitute teach. Mike has remarked:

> I've seen kids who have graduated from your program come into
> Sullivan and substitute, and they are full of exuberance. They feel
> comfortable. They come in with the attitude, "I've got something to
> offer you." Other more traditional subs seem to keep the children
> controlled for the day. They have a different outlook.

Other graduates go on to full-time jobs but they keep in touch. During the holidays each year I often receive cards from former students.

Vanessa, one of my first twenty-five volunteers at Sullivan in 1989, student-taught at Sullivan and then worked with fifth graders there for her Senior Partnership. She now teaches near Hartford, Connecticut with some tough inner-city kids. Here is a note she sent me at Christmas:

> Dr. Allen,
>
> . . . . It is now midnight that I write to you—reason being I just
> finished my lessons for tomorrow. This night is no exception. After
> my college courses (I'm going for my masters in Art Education) I hit
> the books. I love it! . . . I am putting 100% into my job. These city
> kids need me and I often get goose bumps when I hear some of their
> stories or how they have been affected by me.
>
> My most recent of many stories is about Greg—a notoriously
> trouble-making kid. Well lately he has truly been trying so I decided
> to send home a note explaining his effort. The next day when I
> asked Greg about his family's response, he said, "My mom freaked
> and my dad took me out to eat at Ponderosa!"
>
> I've done everything from give a police report for breaking up a
> fight when a parent jumped my student to teaching POETRY! I'm
> already buying tissues for all the tears of joy and sadness I'll experi-
> ence when they leave in June! Hope all is well with you.
>
> Love, Laughter, and Sunshine,
Vanessa

Vanessa is one of the many who is making and will continue to make a difference. I am proud of her, as I am of so many of the other university students. Their efforts have inched children closer to more literate lives.

There is an old African proverb that states, "It takes an entire village to raise a child." The students and professors at the university, the teachers and children in the schools, and the folks in the community agencies are part of this village. We are raising the children to be literate and we are doing it together.

Professional References

Books and Articles

Atwell, Nancie. 1987. *In the Middle*. Portsmouth, NH: Boynton/Cook-Heinemann.

Benard, Bonnie. 1993. Fostering Resiliency in Kids. *Educational Leadership* 51 (3):44–48.

Bissex, Glenda. 1987. Wonderings to Pursue. In *Literacy in Process*, ed. Brenda Miller Power and Ruth Hubbard. Portsmouth, NH: Heinemann.

Calkins, Lucy McCormick. 1994. *The Art of Teaching Writing*. Portsmouth, NH: Heinemann.

————. 1990. *Living Between the Lines*. Portsmouth, NH: Heinemann.

Clinchy, Evan. 1993. Needed: A Clinton Crusade for Quality and Equity. *Phi Delta Kappan* 74 (8):605–612.

College Enrollment by Racial and Ethnic Group. 1994. *Chronicle of Higher Education Almanac* (September 1):15.

Darling-Hammond, Linda. 1993. Reframing the School Reform Agenda. *Phi Delta Kappan* (74)10:753–761.

Durkin, Dolores. 1981. What Is the Value of the New Interest in Reading Comprehension? *Language Arts* 58 (1):23–43.

Eitzen, D. Stanley. 1992. Problem Students: The Sociocultural Roots. *Phi Delta Kappan* 73 (8):584–590.

Evangelauf, Jean. 1993. Number of Minority Students in College Rose by 9% from 1990–1991, U.S. Reports. *Chronicle of Higher Education* (January 10).

Fulwiler, Toby. 1991. Student Journals. In *Literacy in Process*, ed. Brenda Miller Power and Ruth Hubbard. Portsmouth, NH: Heinemann.

Goodlad, John I. 1990. *Teachers for Our Nation's Schools*. San Francisco: Jossey-Bass.

Graves, Donald H. 1983. *Writing: Teachers and Children at Work*. Portsmouth, NH: Heinemann.

Haberman, Martin. 1987. *Recruiting and Selecting Teachers for Urban Schools*. Reston, VA: Association of Teacher Educators.

Hansen, Jane. 1987. *When Writers Read*. Portsmouth, NH: Heinemann.

Heath, Shirley Brice. 1983. *Ways With Words: Language, Life, and Work in Communities and Classrooms*. Cambridge, UK: Cambridge University Press.

Higher Education Act of 1965 as Amended. U.S. Department of Education, Student Literacy Corps Program CFDA 84.219A Award Number P219A20011.

Higher Education Act of 1965 as Amended. U.S. Department of Education, Student Literacy and Mentoring Corps Program P219A30051–93.

Hodgkinson, Harold. 1993. American Education: The Good, the Bad and the Task. *Phi Delta Kappan* 74 (8):619–623.

May, Frank B. 1994. *Reading As Communication*. New York: Macmillan.

————. 1990. *Reading As Communication*. Columbus, OH: Merrill.

Newkirk, Thomas and Patricia McLure. 1993. *Listening In*. Portsmouth, NH: Heinemann.

Pearson, P. David. 1979. *The Effect of Background Knowledge on Young Children's Comprehension of Explicit and Implicit Information*. Champaign, IL: Center for the Study of Reading, University of Illinois.

Rhodes, Warren, A. and Waln K. Brown, eds. 1991. *Why Some Children Succeed Despite the Odds*. New York: Praeger.

Rose, Mike. 1989. *Lives on the Boundary*. New York: Penguin.

Sirotnik, Kenneth A. 1990. Society, Schooling, Teaching, and Preparing to Teach. In *The Moral Dimensions of Teaching*, ed. John I. Goodlad, Roger Soder, and Kenneth A. Sirotnik. San Francisco: Jossey-Bass.

Smith, Frank. 1992. Learning to Read: The Never-Ending Debate. *Phi Delta Kappan* 73 (8):432–441.

Smith, Joan K. and Glenn L. Smith. 1994. *Education Today The Foundations of a Profession*. New York: St. Martin's Press.

Stevens, Linda J. and Marianne Price. 1992. Meeting the Challenge of Educating Children at Risk. *Phi Delta Kappan* 74 (1):18–23.

Taylor, Denny. 1989. Toward a Unified Theory of Literacy Learning and Instructional Practices. *Phi Delta Kappan* 71 (3):184–193.

Westheimer, Joel and Joseph Kahne. 1993. Building School Communities: An Experience-Based Model. *Phi Delta Kappan* 75 (4):324–328.

Wiggins, Grant. 1993. Assessment: Authenticity, Context, and Validity. *Phi Delta Kappan* 75 (3):200–214.

Wolf, Kenneth. 1991. The Schoolteacher's Portfolio: Issues in Design, Implementation, and Evaluation. *Phi Delta Kappan* 73 (2):129–136.

Zemelman, Steven, Harvey Daniels, and Arthur Hyde. 1993. *Best Practice New Standards for Teaching and Learning in America's Schools*. Portsmouth, NH: Heinemann.

Videos

Calkins, Lucy, Shelley Harwayne, and Alex Mitchell. *The Writing Workshop: A World of Difference*. Portsmouth, NH: Heinemann.

Hansen, Jane, and Donald H. Graves. *The Writing and Reading Process*. Portsmouth, NH: Heinemann.

Books for Beginning Readers

Alphabet Knowledge

The Alphabet Pals' Surprise. World Book, Inc.

Berenstain, Stan and Jan Berenstain. 1971. *The "B" Book*. Random House.

Blake, Quentin. 1989. *Quentin Blake's ABC*. Alfred A. Knopf.

Boynton, Sandra. 1984. *A to Z*. Simon & Schuster.

Carter, David A. 1994. *Alpha Bugs*. Simon & Schuster.

Chwast, Seymour. 1969. *Still Another Alphabet Book*. McGraw Hill.

Eastman, P.D. 1974. *The Alphabet Book*. Random House.

Eichenberg, Fritz. 1980. *Ape in the Cape*. Harcourt, Brace, Jovanovich.

MacDonald, Suse. 1992. *Alphabatics*. Macmillan Child Group.

Mayer, Mercer. 1978. *Little Monster's Alphabet Book*. Western Publishing Company.

Merriam, Eve. 1987. *Halloween ABC*. Macmillan Child Group.

Ryden, Hope. 1988. *Wild Animals of America ABC*. Dutton's Children's Books.

Seuss, Dr. 1991. *ABC*. Random House.

Colors and Shapes

Crews, Donald. 1978. *Freight Train*. Greenwillow Books.

Dudko, Maryann. 1993. *Barney's Color Surprise*. The Lyons Group.

Counting

Adams, Pam. 1979. *There Were 10 In Bed*. Child's Play International.

Bucknall, Caroline. 1989. *One Bear All Alone*. Dial Books for Young Readers.

Crews, Donald. 1986. *Ten Black Dots*. Greenwillow.

D'Andrea, Deborah Bennett. 1991. *Count with Me 1,2,3*. Picture Me Books, Inc.

Hutchins, Pat. 1986. *The Doorbell Rang*. Greenwillow Children's Books.

Lambert, Jonathan. 1992. *Numbers*. Longmeadow Press.

Mayer, Mercer. 1978. *Little Monster's Counting Book*. Western Publishing Company, Inc.

Noll, Sally. 1984. *Off and Counting*. Greenwillow.

Viorst, Judith. 1972. *Alexander and The Terrible, Horrible, No Good, Very Bad Day*. Atheneum.

Xiong, Blia, Cathy Spagnoli, and Nancy Hom. 1989. *Nine in One Grr!Grr!* Children's Book Press.

Days of the Week

Hooper, Meredith. 1985. *Seven Eggs.* Harper.

Rockwell, Anne. 1989. *Bear Child's Book of Special Days.* Dutton Children's Books.

Dr. Seuss Books

Seuss, Dr. 1957. *The Cat in the Hat.* Random House.

————. 1960. *Green Eggs and Ham.* Random House.

————. 1960. *One Fish Two Fish Red Fish Blue Fish.* Random House.

————. 1963. *Hop on Pop.* Random House.

————. 1968. *The Foot Book.* Random House.

————. 1970. *Mr. Brown Can Moo! Can You?* Random House.

————. 1971. *The Lorax.* Random House.

————. 1979. *Oh Say Can You Say?* Random House.

Dinosaurs

Cole, Joanna. 1974. *Dinosaur Story.* Morrow Junior Books.

Crozat, Francois. 1990. *I Am a Big Dinosaur.* Barron's Educational Series, Incorporated.

Donnelly, Liza. 1987. *Dinosaur Day.* Scholastic, Incorporated.

————. 1991. *Dinosaur Garden.* Scholastic, Incorporated.

Hoff, Syd. 1993. *Danny and the Dinosaur.* Harper Collins.

Kroll, Steven. 1976. *The Tyrannosaurus Game.* Holiday.

Easy Reading

Barton, Byron. 1972. *Where's Al?* Seabury Press.

Cowley, Joy. *Big and Little.* The Wright Group.

————. *Dinner.* The Wright Group.

————. *Don't You Laugh At Me.* The Wright Group.

————. *Goodbye.* The Wright Group.

————. *Good for You.* The Wright Group.

————. *I Can Jump*. The Wright Group.

————. *Ice Cream,* The Wright Group.

————. *Little Brother*. The Wright Group.

————. *A Monster Sandwich*. The Wright Group.

————. *Mrs. Wishy Washy*. The Wright Group.

————. *Nowhere and Nothing*. The Wright Group.

————. *Quack, Quack, Quack!* The Wright Group.

————. *Tess and Paddy*. The Wright Group.

————. *The Giant's Boy*. The Wright Group.

————. *The Secret of Spooky House*. The Wright Group.

————. *What Would You Like?* The Wright Group.

————. *When Itchy Witchy Sneezes*. The Wright Group.

Cutting, Jillian. *At School*. The Wright Group.

————. *The Birthday Party*. The Wright Group.

————. *I Am*. The Wright Group.

————. *My Family*. The Wright Group.

————. *Our Grandad*. The Wright Group.

————. *To School*. The Wright Group.

Dabcovich, Lydia. 1982. *Sleepy Bear*. Dutton.

Darrin, Bobby and Jean Murray. 1993. *Splish, Splash*. Leonard, Hal Corporation.

Ginsburg, Mirra. 1975. *Good Morning Chick*. Macmillan.

Halpern, Shari. 1992. *My River*. MacMillan Child Group.

Hill, Eric. 1980. *Where's Spot?* Putnam's.

Keller, Holly. 1988. *Geraldine's Big Snow*. Greenwillow.

LeSieg, Theodore. 1972. *In a People House*. Random House.

Maris, Ron. 1985. *Is Anyone Home?* Greenwillow.

McMillan, Bruce. 1983. *Here a Chick, There a Chick*. Lothrop.

Reit, Seymour. 1990. *The Flying School Bus*. Western Publishing Company, Incorporated.

Sage, James. 1990. *To Sleep*. Macmillan.

Shaw, Charles Green. 1947. *It Looked Like Spilt Milk*. Harper.

Shaw, Nancy. 1986. *Sheep in a Jeep*. Houghton.

Shiffman, Lena. 1992. *My First Book of Words*. Scholastic, Inc.

Westcott, Nadine Bernard. 1987. *Getting Up*. Little.

Halloween

Alley, Robert. 1982. *The Ghost in Dobb's Diner*. Parents Magazine Press.

de Paola, Tomie. 1991. *My First Halloween*. The Putnam Publishing Group.

Gantos, Jack. 1986. *Rotten Ralph's Trick or Treat!* Houghton.

Pienkowski, Jan. 1979. *Haunted House*. Dutton Children's Books.

Prelutsky, Jack. 1987. *It's Halloween*. Scholastic, Incorporated.

Schwartz, Alvin. 1993. *Ghosts*. Harper Collins Children's Books.

Picture Books/Good Illustrations

Allen, Pamela. 1983. *Who Sank the Boat?* Coward.

Barton, Byron. 1992. *I Want to be an Astronaut*. Harper Collins

Brown, Margaret Wise. 1934. *Goodnight Moon*. Harper.

Brown, Ruth. 1993. *One Stormy Night*. Dutton Children's Books.

Carle, Eric. 1969. *The Very Hungry Caterpillar*. Collins-World.

————. 1971. *Do You Want To Be My Friend?* Crowell.

————. 1973. *Have You Seen My Cat?*. Watts.

————. 1977. *The Grouchy Ladybug*. Crowell.

————. 1975. *The Mixed-Up Chameleon*. Crowell.

————. 1985. *The Very Busy Spider*. Philomel.

————. 1990. *The Very Quiet Cricket*. Putnam.

Cohen, Daniel. 1993. *Prehistoric Animals*. Dell Publishing Company, Inc.

Cossi, Olga. 1989. *Gus the Bus*. Scholastic.

Crews, Donald. 1980. *Truck*. Greenwillow.

Crozat, Francois. 1989. *I Am a Little Rabbit*. Barron's Educational Series, Inc.

Day, Alexandra. 1985. *Good Dog, Carl*. Green Tiger Press.

————. 1988. *Frank and Ernest*. Scholastic.

dePaola, Tomie. 1991. *Pancakes for Breakfast*. Scholastic.

Handford, Martin. 1987. *Where's Waldo?* Little.

Henkes, Kevin. 1989. *Shhhh*. Greenwillow.

Hillert, Margaret. 1963. *The Three Bears*. Follet.

Johnson, Crockett. 1960. *A Picture for Harold's Room*. Harper.

Maris, Ron. 1983. *My Book*. Watts.

Mayer, Mercer. 1969. *Frog Where Are You?* Dial Press.

————. 1975. *Just for You*. Golden Press.

Oppenheim, Joanne. 1967. *Have You Seen Trees?* Addison-Wesley.

Robbins, Ken. 1991. *Bridges*. Dial Books for Young Readers.

Sendak, Maurice. 1963. *Where the Wild Things Are.* Harper.

————. 1970. *In The Night Kitchen.* Harper.

Tucker, Sian. 1994. *Animals.* Simon & Schuster Trade.

Wallner, John. 1986. *Old MacDonald Had a Farm.* Dutton.

Walsh, Ellen Stoll. 1992. *You Silly Goose.* Harcourt.

Ziefert, Harriet. 1986. *Keeping Daddy Awake on the Way Home from the Beach.* Harper.

Pop-Up Books

Drinan, Neil. 1992. *The Boy and the Horse.* Child's Play International.

Pelham, David. 1991. *Sam's Sandwich.* Dutton Children's Press.

Shapiro, Arnold. 1994. *The Neighbor Game: A Pop-Up-Figure-It-Out-Book.* Dial Books for Young Readers.

Rhyme and/or Repetition

Adams, Pam. 1979. *This is the House that Jack Built.* Child's Play International.

————. 1990. *There Was an Old Lady Who Swallowed a Fly.* Child's Play International.

Bourgeois, Paulette. 1987. *Franklin in the Dark.* Scholastic, Incorporated.

Cameron, Polly. 1961. *"I Can't," Said the Ant.* Scholastic, Incorporated.

Charles, Donald. 1978. *Time to Rhyme With Calico Cat.* Children's Press.

Cristelow, Eileen. 1991. *Five Little Monkeys Sitting in a Tree.* Houghton.

Frith, Michael. 1973. *I'll Teach My Dog 100 Words.* Random House.

Gelman, Rita Golden. 1993. *Hello, Cat You Need a Hat.* Scholastic, Incorporated.

Hutchins, Pat. 1983. *You'll Soon Grow Into Them.* Greenwillow.

Leonard, Marcia, and Diane Palmisciano. 1988. *Follow That Car.* Bantam.

Martin, Bill, Jr. 1992. *Brown Bear, Brown Bear, What Do You See?* Holt.

Mayer, Mercer. 1975. *Just for You.* Golden Press.

Mayer, Mercer. 1987. *There's an Alligator Under My Bed.* Dial Press.

Minarik, Else Holmelund. 1957. *Little Bear.* Harper.

Pelham, David. 1994. *Sam's Snacks.* Dutton Children's Books.

Prelutsky, Jack. 1986. *Read Aloud Rhymes for the Very Young.* A. Knopf.

Quackenbush, Robert. 1981. *Henry's Awful Mistake.* Parents Magazine Press.

Ross, Tony. 1984. *I'm Coming to Get You.* Dial Press.

Sendak, Maurice. 1962. *Chicken Soup with Rice.* Harper.

Silverstein, Shel. 1986. *Where the Sidewalk Ends*. Dell Publishing Company, Inc.

Tarfuri, Nancy. 1986. *Have You Seen My Duckling?* Viking Children's Books.

Trelo, Jim. 1973. *Read Aloud Rhymes for the Very Young*. Dial Press.

Wells, Rosemary. 1973. *Noisy Nora*. Dial Press.

Williams, Linda and Megan Lloyd. 1986. *The Little Old Lady Who Was Not Afraid of Anything*. Crowell.

Story Line/Characters

Aardema, Verna. 1984. *Oh Kojo! How Could You?* Dial.

Allard, Harry. 1989. *Miss Nelson Has a Field Day*. Houghton Mifflin.

Asch, Frank. 1984. *Moongame*. Prentice-Hall.

Berenstein, Jan and Stan Berenstain. 1987. *The Berenstein Bears Go Out for the Team*. Random House.

Berenstain, Stan and Jan Berenstain. 1988. *The Berenstain Bears and the Double Dare*. Random House.

Biro, Val. 1990. *Jack and the Beanstalk*. Oxford University Press.

————. 1991. *Three Little Pigs*. Oxford University Press.

Bonsall, Crosby. 1974. *And I Mean It, Stanley*. Harper.

Brett, Jan. 1990. *The Mitten*. Putnam.

Cole, Joanna. 1986. *This Is the Place for Me*. Scholastic.

Cole, Joanna, and Dirk Zimmer. 1983. *Bony Legs*. Four Winds Press.

dePaola, Tomie. 1987. *Bill and Pete Go Down the Nile River*. Putnam's.

Disney, Walt. 1979. *Snow White and the Seven Dwarfs*. Viking.

Eastman, P. D. 1960. *Are You My Mother?*. Random House.

Freeman, Don. 1988. *Corduroy*. Puffin.

Henkes, Kevin. 1989. *Jessica*. Greenwillow.

Hoban, Lillian. 1990. *Silly Tilly's Thanksgiving Dinner*. Harper & Row.

Hoban, Russel. 1968. *A Birthday for Francis*. Harper.

Hogrogian, Nonny. 1981. *Cinderella*. Greenwillow.

Hutchins, Pat. 1978. *Happy Birthday, Sam*. Greenwillow.

Kano, Keiko. 1987. *Kitten up a Tree*. Knopf.

Kraus, Robert. 1970. *Whose Mouse Are You?* Macmillan.

Lionni, Leo. 1993. *Frederick*. Books for Young Readers.

Mayer, Mercer. 1968. *There's a Nightmare in My Closet*. Dial Press.

McLeod, Emily. 1975. *The Bear's Bicycle*. Little.

McPhail, David. 1987. *Emma's Pet*. Dutton.

Moffett, Martha. 1972. *A Flower Pot Is Not a Hat*. Dutton.

Noble, Trinka Hakes. 1980. *The Day Jimmy's Boa Ate the Wash*. Dial Press.

Oxenbury, Helen. 1983. *The Dancing Class*. Dial Press.

Potter, Beatrix. 1979. *The Tale of Peter Rabbit*. Troll Associates.

Rey, Margaret and H. A. Rey. 1941. *Curious George*. Houghton Mifflin.

———. 1990. *Curious George at the Railroad Station*. Scholastic.

Rubel, Nicole. 1988. *It Came From the Swamp*. Dial Press.

Sadler, Marilyn. 1984. *The Very Bad Bunny*. Beginner Books.

Stevenson, Peter. 1993. *The Gingerbread Man*. Ladybird Books.

Thaler, Mike. 1993. *Never Mail an Elephant*. Troll Associates.

Turpin, Lorna. 1991. *The Sultan's Snakes*. Child's Play International.

Tyler, Linda. 1988. *The Sick in Bed Birthday*. Viking Kestrel.

———. 1989. *My Brother Oscar Thinks He Knows It All*. Viking Kestrel.

Watson, Joy. 1993. *Grandpa's Slippers*. Scholastic, Incorporated.

West, Cindy. 1993. *The Three Bears*. Western Publishing Company, Incorporated.

Other Books for Young Readers

Aliki. 1962. *My Five Senses*. Crowell.

Asch, Frank. 1979. *Popcorn*. Parents.

———. 1985. *Bear Shadow*. Prentice-Hall.

———. 1980. *The Last Puppy*. Prentice-Hall.

Aylesworth, Jim. 1992. *Old Black Fly*. Holt, Henry, and Company, Inc.

Bailey, Debbie. 1991. *Shoes*. Firefly Books, Limited.

———. 1993. *Brothers*. Firefly Books, Limited.

Baker, Jeannie. 1988. *Where the Forest Meets the Sea*. Greenwillow Books.

Bancroft, Henrietta, and Richard Van Guilder. 1963. *Animals in Winter*. Crowell.

Boynton, Sandra. 1982. *Opposites*. Simon & Schuster.

———. 1984. *Blue Hat, Green Hat*. Simon & Schuster Trade.

Brown, Margaret Wise. 1943. *Shhh . . . Bang*. Harper.

———. 1944. *Red Light Green Light*. Doubleday.

———. 1950. *The Dream Book*. Random House.

Fleming, Denise. 1993. *In the Small, Small Pond*. Holt, Henry, and Company, Inc.

Garcia, Gloria. 1990a. *Flying High*. Child's Play International.

———. 1990b. *A Life on an Ocean Wave*. Child's Play International.

Gordon, Sharon. 1981. *Maxwell Mouse*. Troll Associates.

Gretz, Susanna. 1988. *Roger Loses His Marbles*. Dial Press.

Holladay, John. 1992. *What's Wrong at the Winter Carnival?* Smithmark Publishers, Inc.

Hill, Eric. 1985. *Spot on the Farm*. Putnam's.

Hirschi, Ron. 1990. *Winter*. Dutton.

Hoff, Syd. 1960. *Who Will Be My Friends?* Harper.

Hutchins, Pat. 1975. *Don't Forget the Bacon*. Greenwillow.

Keats, Ezra Jack. 1964. *Whistle for Willie*. Viking.

Kraus, Robert. 1986. *Where Are You Going Little Mouse?* Greenwillow.

Lavie, Arlette. 1990. *Half a World Away*. Child's Play International.

Leigh, Tom. 1983. *The Sesame Street Word Book*. Western Publishing Company.

LeSieg, Theodore. 1976. *Hooper Humperdink, Not Him!* Random House.

Lionni, Leo. 1994. *An Extraordinary Egg*. Books for Young Readers.

The Little Red Hen. 1985. Scholastic, Inc.

Mayer, Mercer. 1978. *Little Monster at Home*. Golden Press.

Medearis, Angela. 1993. *Dancing with the Indians: A Reading Rainbow Review*. Holiday House, Incorporated.

Menzel, Barbara. 1982. *Would You Rather*. Human Sciences Press, Incorporated.

Paris, Pat. 1989. *This Old Man*. Barron's Educational Series, Incorporated.

Perrault, Charles. adapt. by Lorinda Bryan Cauley. 1986. *Puss and Boots*. Harcourt.

Pienkowski, Jan. 1992. *Doorbell*. Price Stern Sloan.

Pinkwater, Daniel. 1983. *I Was a Second Grade Werewolf*. Dutton.

Raschka, Chris. 1993. *Yo! Yes?* Orchard Books.

Rylant, Cynthia. 1982. *When I Was Young in the Mountains*. Dutton.

Seuling. 1976. *The Teeny Tiny Woman*. Viking.

Silverstein, Shel. 1969. *A Giraffe and a Half*. Harper.

Slobodkin, Louis. 1959. *Trick or Treat*. Macmillan.

Tafuri, Nancy. 1987. *In a Red House*. Greenwillow.

Turkle, Brinton. 1976. *Deep in the Forest*. Dutton Children's Books.

Udry. 1956. *A Tree Is Nice*. Harper.

Wells, Rosemary. 1976. *Max's Bedtime*. Dial Books for Young Readers.

Wood, Leslie. 1987. *The Frog and the Fly*. Oxford University Press.